# Amazing Love

The Life Journey of a man,
Formerly A "Dead Man
Walking;"
Billy Hall

By Billy Hall

Published by:
Rehoboth Media
429 N Palm Ave. Unit A
Alhambra, CA 91801

# DEDICATION

To my Lord and Savior Jesus Christ, Who wonderfully broke my stony heart with His Amazing Love.....

To my dad, for pointing me to Christ by living Christ-like before me.....

To the many people, who God has invested in my life - this story is <u>your</u> story too.....

LASTLY, to each of you who read this book, for whomever you are and wherever you are in life - God is waiting to begin a <u>Journey of Adventure</u> with you.

For you see this story is only a preview of coming attractions for your life when you <u>personally</u> experience Christ's Amazing Love for you!

# FOREWARD

Within our history lies our hope. This is never more true than when we see someone's life unfold before us. Bill (Billy) Hall's life is such a tremendous story of God's Love. Unassuming like the cover of a small book, his life unfolds. From prison bars to the stars God has taken Billy. Know this, that what God has done for one, He can do for you.

I pray this story of redemption moves you as much as it has me. From seed faith to the nations of the world. This is the kind of book you want to read and pass on to a friend.

Yours For Revival
Pastor Johnny Dorris

## TABLE OF CONTENTS

| | |
|---|---|
| DEDICATION ........................... | 2 |
| FOREWARD............................ | 3 |
| INTRODUCTION...................... | 5 |

**CHAPTER ONE**
    *The Early Years* ...............  7
**CHAPTER TWO**
    *The Few - The Proud* .......  21
**CHAPTER THREE**
    *Life Without the Corps*.......  33
**CHAPTER FOUR**
    *DEAD MAN WALKING*.......  43
**CHAPTER FIVE**
    *The Son Has Set You Free..*  57
**CHAPTER SIX**
    *Called To Serve*...................  69
**CHAPTER SEVEN**
    *Out Of My Tree*....................  85
**CHAPTER EIGHT**
    *Now What?*..........................  93
**CHAPTER NINE**
    *Here Comes The Promise!*...  107
**CHAPTER TEN**
    *The Birth Of Joanna*............  119
**CHAPTER ELEVEN**
    *Out Of Ethiopia*....................  125
**CHAPTER TWELVE**
    *What Has God Done?*.........  131

## INTRODUCTION

The corners of the Prime Minister's mouth showed the slightest hint of a smile as his eyes fixed on a distant stare. His sense of joy at the recent turn of events was nearly irrepressible as he reviewed the amazing experiences of his life. It all made sense now; the rejection by his family, the season of slavery, the false accusations by people in influential positions, the long sorrow filled years in prison, the unbelievable dreams of an impossible future, sudden freedom with stellar promotion, and at long last the healing of all the relationships with his entire family.

Somehow, he knew deep in his heart, through all the years of his adversity, that THIS day would come. The day when God's dreams, plans and visions for his life would finally come to pass. Single tears of joy ran from the corner of his eyes and down his cheek halfway as he reminisced.

The only visible reminder of his suffering - the scars on his ankles from the chains of imprisonment. To him - a small price to pay for the survival of his family, a nation within a nation, Israel. His life's terrible experiences had turned out to be

God's instruments of preparation for him to become the uncontested leader of the civilized world - the nation of Egypt.

The man's name was Joseph. He lived thousands of years ago and his story has inspired millions over the millennia.

"That may have happened way back then, but that kind of stuff just doesn't happen to people anymore today;" many people of our generation say, not realizing that God never changes! What God did for Joseph, He wants to do for you today in His own unique way! God has filled human history with people just like Joseph to demonstrate His *Amazing Love* for us.

No matter what your failures, tragedies and traumas, God's *Amazing Love* has a special plan for you to experience His ultimate victory and meaning.

Billy Hall is a primary demonstration to our troubled generation of the extent to which God still goes to add meaning and unspeakable joy to life. The story of Billy Hall is truly the story of God's *Amazing Love* for you!

# CHAPTER ONE

## *The Early Years*

What a year 1948 was! America was on the road to recovery from the close of World War II. Harry Truman was President, Israel became a nation - and on February 26, 1948 I was born to my very proud parents Reba and William Hall. I had an older sister Carol Ann, and eventually a younger sister, Patty, came along to complete the family. Everyone at our house loved God and was a Christian - with the exception of me.

Every Sunday we all packed up the family car and commuted to the church where my sisters and I split off and went off to Sunday School. I complained about Church, "Daddy, why do I have to go to Sunday School?" My Dad consistently replied, "as long as you're under my roof, young man, you will go to church!" My Daddy was big on consistency!

As I reflect on these, my earliest years, I remember clearly as a little boy growing up in the shadow of the greatest hero anyone could possibly have, my dad. He was truly amazing to me. In my mind, he was never 5 years old, he was born an adult. He always had all the answers to my questions. He was a rock for me to rely upon. Honesty and humility were the portrait of his lifestyle. To this day, I know my dad would rather die than tell a lie. One night as a little boy, I lay awake thinking what would happen to me if he ever died. I just couldn't see how I could ever live without him.

I thought about this a lot because my daddy was more than just a hero to me . . . he was a United States Marine!

I was very active as a young boy growing up in Oceanside, California. My dad was stationed at Camp Pendleton and we lived in the Starlight Housing area of what was then called "off-base housing." All of us children would play together and use our father's rank as the measure of authority among us.

When my dad left for the Korean War in 1950 I was just two years old. I remember dragging his rifle down the driveway with his helmet hanging on my neck. I was so proud that my daddy was going off to the war. I didn't understand why mommy was crying so much. Each week my sisters and I would sit around mommy and write a letter to daddy. I remember how mommy would cry as she folded the letters and placed them in the mail.

When the announcement came three years later that my dad's division was coming home I was so happy. We all went to the airport that night and watched all the planes land and unload the hundreds of Marines. They came all night long. I looked so carefully at each man. As I looked, my mind was reeling with the questions a little boy's heart could barely hold. "Where's my daddy?" "Why can't I see him?" The last plane landed early in the morning and my daddy wasn't among the Marines who came off the plane. A neighbor of ours drove us all back to our house as I cried myself to sleep asking God "Please God, don't let my daddy be dead!"

To my great joy, the very next morning I was awakened by the sound of an electric shaver, and I caught the faint scent of my favorite aroma, my daddy's Mennen Skin Bracer, and my heart knew what it meant...... I ran into the bathroom screaming with joy, "Daddy, oh Daddy" hugging his leg. Oh I was so happy - and relieved.

We moved to South Gate, a suburb of Los Angeles shortly after this and it was here at the age of 7 that I had my first intimate encounter with God. I was sitting in my Sunday School Class and I heard a voice behind me say, "One day <u>You</u> will preach My Gospel." I turned around to see who was talking to me but no one was there. As a little boy I thought I was just hearing things..... (I was, I was hearing God!).

I was also ready for public school. In my second grade class, the teacher has taken us to the La Brea Tar Pits, on a class field trip.

I was so impressed that when I got home I decided to make my own La Brea Tar Pit in the back yard. I dug a pit that covered my head. Then I filled it with water and dirt and let it become muddy like a "tar pit."

That night, as I was playing outside, my dad came looking for me. "Billy, Billy, where are you . . . . Billyyyyy" and then I heard him cry out in pain as he sank into my "tar pit." I thought, "Oh no, I am really gonna get it now!"

I ran into the house to eat dinner and as I sat there eating he announced that after I finished, I was going to get a serious spanking. I just knew it was so.

After dinner, I wandered outside to the back porch, and there I looked up at the stars. I began to pray; "If you can hear me up there, please send a space ship for me and take me away." And "God, please make my Daddy not be so angry with me, and help him not to spank me very hard. I'm so sorry God!"

As I turned from praying that moment, my eyes caught a glimpse of my dad looking at me through the curtain of the door where he was crying; my daddy had heard all that I had said. That moment of time really made a strong impact on me, because my dad was a man full of compassion. We hugged each other and I went off to bed with a broken heart, for what I had unintentionally done to my dad.

During the first four years of elementary school my mother became very sick. She became ill to the point that she was confined to her bed.

My sisters and I took on the household duties of cleaning, and shopping for groceries. My older sister Carol Ann actually became the leader for my younger sister and I, and she was the boss. It seemed that whenever confusion or panic would come into our lives, Carol Ann would be there to calm the panic and clear away the confusion for Patty and I. I'm sure that I contributed the least to the daily chores of the house.

During this time I learned to cook, iron, clean and shop for groceries for myself and the family.

We took turns making sack lunches for each other for school. We really liked it when it was Carol Ann's turn. She was the oldest and her sandwiches were great! My lunches however were not as good, peanut butter and jelly was about it.

I made my first family breakfast on Saturday morning, when I was 7. I was so proud of my pancakes. My dad took one bite and said "That's real good Billy, that will probably last me until dinner tonight." I had put too much flour into the mix.....

We had such great times in the evenings watching television with mom and dad: Ellery Queen Mysteries, Perry Mason, Ozzie & Harriet, Father Knows Best, Life of Riley, The Honeymooners, Paladin, Gunsmoke and the Lone Ranger. Perry

Mason and Ellery Queen were my dad's favorites.

In 4th grade my behavior in school became intolerable. It seemed that the more I tried to be good the more trouble I got into. My fights with the "hall monitors" and disobedience to the teacher brought me into the Principal's office for the last time. The result was that I was expelled from the Los Angeles Unified School District. I really upset my dad.

He took me to a private school, St. Paul's Lutheran Elementary School. Unknown to me, the school's principal had advised him that the school had a policy of using corporal punishment to ensure student discipline and conformity to the school's rules of conduct. The classroom was divided into two sections, one for the 5th grade and one for the 6th grade. By mistake, I sat in the 6th grade side.

I started off on the wrong foot. The first week I disturbed the class every day. I didn't do my homework, I told the teacher that I didn't care what she thought, I put thumbtacks on her chair; and all she did was open her top drawer and write something on

a pad, and quietly close her drawer again. I thought this was very strange.
On the following Friday, the Principal, Mrs. Bissel, visited our classroom. She was about 6'2" and weighed about 220 pounds. She was a BIG woman.

When she turned to the teacher she was handed a clipboard with that mysterious pad of paper from the teacher's top drawer. When she read aloud, "Billy Hall, 49 demerits," there was dead silence.

All the students put their hands over their ears, some put their heads down; but I felt pretty proud! I didn't know what a demerit was, I thought it was some kind of a reward. She commanded "Come to the front of the class!" I thought, here's my chance to show off!
Then she said "Grab your ankles!" I said "What?"

Then she put her hand firmly on my neck and pushed me down. When I grabbed my ankles she pulled out from her back pocket an aluminum ping pong paddle with holes in it; the silence was ominous.

The first crack made me dizzy and caused the girls to start crying. Although I bit my lip the tears still rolled down my cheek, 48 more strokes......

I walked back to my seat but I couldn't sit down all the way on my seat.

The next student who was called had 2 demerits; and all the others had either 1 or 2 demerits. The next Friday when Mrs Bissel came to visit our classroom, Billy Hall's name was not on the list at all! I was reformed. My grades at the end of the semester were all A's with 2 B's. The principal suggested to my dad that I stay on the $6^{th}$ grade side since my grades were so good.

After that school year was over we moved to Pasadena and I returned to the public school system, attending McKinley Junior High School, being a rebel again. Since I was the smallest boy in my class, I compensated by being the wildest. When I was not tearing the school bus apart, seat by seat, I did other things to gain attention. I remember walking on the dangerously narrow ledge of the second story, just outside the window of my French class to gain the terrified attention of the girls inside.

In school I was a different person than I was at home. My mother had become worse in her illness and as a result, my behavior became worse. I felt the need to escape the responsibilities that had become part of my daily life. I decided to run away from home at the age of 13. I hitch-hiked down to Laguna Beach and slept under a pier there. During the day I obtained food from the local stores and stored my supplies up on the inside of the pier pilings. There it all was: jars of peanut butter, mayonnaise, mustard, bologna, cheese, bread, cigarettes and sodas. It looked like a little store.

One day a lady saw me coming out from under the pier and she asked me "What are you doing under there?" I told her that I was just hanging around. With an understanding look, she led me off to her house where she gave me her mattress off of her lawn chair to sleep on at night.

Not many weeks later, I returned home. Dad's reception was really cold. When he came home and saw me he simply said, "Oh, you're home now." For three days he acted as if I wasn't even there. When I talked to him he didn't respond. He talked to my sisters as if I wasn't there, totally ignoring me.

This was the dreaded "silent treatment" and it was absolutely unbearable. I finally exploded, "Please, beat me or yell at me, but whatever you do please don't ignore me anymore! He began talking with me on the fourth day.

In 1962 I managed to get promoted to $10^{th}$ grade where I attended John Muir High School. I still had an enormous "chip on my shoulder" from being so small. One day as I was walking the 4-mile trek home from school, I heard a voice behind me say "One day you will preach My Gospel." Startled, I turned to see who was behind me, but there was no one. I instantly remembered these same words that were spoken to me when I was 7 years old in South Gate. How strange!

I was looking for a place to fit in and I really liked the surfer crowd. I really enjoyed body surfing.

I had become an adept crowd-pleaser. I had to be one way to please this crowd. I had to be another way to please that crowd. Most important, I had to remember who I should be around each crowd. At school I threw myself into the sports program. I had played class "B" Football for only two games when the coach begged me to resign. I was so small that he was afraid I would be seriously hurt. You see, I was 4'11" and weighed 97 pounds and the next largest guy on our team was 5'7" and weighed 150 pounds. The coach said it was true that I ran fast; but if the other team ever got a hold of me I would be hurt really bad.

So I joined the cross-country team and I did really well. I was also able to participate in every level of the track team; Varsity, B and C teams, because I was so small. I ran the 2 mile, the 1 mile, and the ¾ mile races. I ran 10 to 15 miles each day after school as part of my exercise practice. My friend Ralph, rode his bicycle alongside me constantly prodding and encouraging me. I never took a break! Even on the weekends, I ran around the Rose Bowl at least two times. Because of the long distances that I had been running daily, when it was time to run a race it seemed really short. Winning felt so good!

Toward the end of my senior year, my dad asked me what I wanted to do with my life. I didn't know. He told me to either get a job and move out, or go to college and get a part-time job, so I could start paying rent. "You must learn to be responsible," he said.

Well, I knew my grades were bad all through High School because I had spent most of my time at the beach surfing. My summers had been spent in summer school making up for my failing grades. Because of that, the college option was out, and my chances of getting a job were slim to none. I started to think about joining the Marines, because I had wanted to be a Marine since I was 7 years old.

When I told my dad, he laughed. He said I was too weak and would be home crying in a week. I was determined to join up and so one week after graduating from John Muir High School, I joined the Marines, with dad's permission. He was required to sign because I was only 17 years old.

## CHAPTER TWO

*The Few - The Proud*

The man screamed, "Get on the yellow footprints! Move, Move, Move!" I thought, "Why is he is such a hurry?"

This was the "hurry up and wait mental attitude which I was about to learn; part of the "Marine Mentality;" maintaining a state of readiness at all times.

I was laughing at this crazy man screaming at our group until he came up to me and pressed his nose up against my face and screamed, "is something funny, boy!"

I was immediately stunned by the intense feeling of fear and authority of this man.

He continued, "You belong to me for four years. I will be your mother, your father, your sweetheart, your best friend or your worst nightmare, you are mine!" Things could only get worse, and they did. By nightfall some of the guys were crying, "Oh momma, I done died and gone to hell. I'm sure enough in trouble now."

Those 16 weeks of Boot Camp forged our group of 85 boys into the most feared fighting machine in the world; Platoon 352, 1st Battalion, Marine Recruit Deport, San Diego, California.

One particular fellow in our platoon was nicknamed "Crazy." He was from Oklahoma and had been transferred out of several other platoons because of his failure to pass the required tests in Boot Camp. It seemed that he could not graduate.

But the Marine Corps refused to give up on him. He wanted so badly to be a Marine. Our Drill Instructor (DI) Corporal Deziegel, told him in front of all of us, "Other Platoons have failed, but you will graduate from this platoon. Nobody fails in my platoon! Do You Hear Me?" We all screamed "Yes Sir!"

Crazy was special to all of us. We worked to help him, and in the process learned that we were a team, not individuals; and we were only as strong as the weakest man - only as fast as the slowest man. It was to be a very valuable lesson for me as a man.

Because I was so small my DI called me "Little One." Part of our training involved simulated hand-to-hand combat training with a bayonet attached to our rife. This was done with pugle sticks. A pugle stick is a long wooden pole with a pad attached at each end. The object was to bring down the opponent with blows to the body. We all lined up in a single line, one platoon against another platoon; one-on-one. I was relieved when I saw the guy I would be facing was small like me. Then my DI switched me with another guy and I was now going to face a huge guy!

Oh no, I'm going to be crushed! Just as it was my turn, my DI screamed at me "Little One - KILL KILL KILL! I lunged forward and jammed the bottom of the pole into his groin. When he bent down I hit him in the face with the top part of the pole, and it was over for him. I learned that day that the rule in combat was kill or be killed.

Our platoon was the first 100-mile platoon on the depot. We ran before and after each meal. One day Corporal Deziegel proudly challenged anyone to outrun him. I stepped forward and ran behind him for a second lap around the Depot (about 4 ½ miles). He started fading, and I was determined to beat him. He said: "It's OK Little One if you're tired, you can stop anytime!" But I kept running. Shortly after that he said, "Stop running Little One, and that's an order!" From that day on he used me as an example to shame the men who were not physically fit.

When we ate, Corporal Deziegel would stand at the end of the line inspecting what each of us had put on our trays. The heavy guys were not allowed to have any potatoes, gravy, meat, or bread - just vegetables and fruit. My tray was always loaded with meat, potatoes, gravy and bread!

One day we were assembled together at morning formation, and Corporal Deziegel shouted "Private Little One, front and center!" He gave me a blue plastic disk and quietly whispered "This is our Platoon's Luck Piece." I was to keep it secretly and securely at all times - no one was to know about this except him and me. Other DI's and my Commanding Officer tried to get me to tell them about the "lucky piece" but I refused to acknowledge it altogether. Every once and awhile Corporal Deziegel would call me out of formation and quietly say "you still got it Little One?" I would always say, "Yes Sir."

Just before Graduation I got up in the morning and discovered the "lucky piece" was missing under my pillow. That day Corporal Deziegel asked me if I still had it. I lied and said "Yes Sir!" I felt so ashamed and disappointed in myself. He never asked me about the "luck piece" again; and I have always regretted that failure in personal integrity.

When I arrived at the depot I was barely five feet tall and weighed 105 pounds dripping wet. Three months later I was 5 feet 4 inches and weighed 160 pounds. I felt invincible. We all did.

I remember Corporal Deziegel's last command at my graduation, "Platoon 352 - Dismissed!"

We had become men, individually, and a team, corporately. From this time on we were called "Marines."

After another eight weeks of Basic Infantry Training at Camp Pendleton, California I was transferred to my first duty station at Camp Lejeune, North Carolina; all the way on the east coast. I really felt the shock of it when I arrived and didn't know anyone. I was really a junior Marine there. I was assigned to drive the "cattle car" for the transportation of recruits in Camp Geiger. These recruits were graduates from Perris Island, the east coast Boot Camp). The troop handlers accused me of being a "boot," which is to say a new recruit, or a person who is still in boot camp training; and that really irritated me. So I learned the discipline of keeping my mouth shut. And waiting for my time to come when I could go to the fight in Vietnam.

Every week I would ask my Commanding Officer if my orders had come yet. He was really relieved when my orders came 7 weeks later, transferring me to Staging Battalion in Okinawa. I thought, alright, now I'm on my way to where the real action is!

It was at this time I received my first 30 day leave and went home to see my dad and family. He saw me coming up the driveway and ran out of the house to me. Hugging me, he whispered in my ear, "I'm so proud of you son!" I can't remember ever feeling more satisfied with myself than at that moment.

I had finally done something worthwhile with my life; not just for my dad, but for myself. Since I was 7 years old, all I wanted was to be a Marine; one of the few and the finest.

When my friends heard that I was back in town they stopped by my house and wanted me to go out with them and goof around with them. I didn't really feel like doing dumb stuff and I told them so. They were angry and accused me of thinking I was better than them now. There actions seemed so childish to me and I now realized how much I had matured in such a short time. Later on, each of them joined different branches of the military and they experienced the same transformation as I did.

I left for Okinawa early in 1966 and arrived in Vietnam that August. I remember the nauseating stench in the air when I got off the plane. I asked a flight line soldier what the smell was, and he said "those body bags are full of body parts of dead men." It was then that the reality of war hit me like a brick in the face.

I was assigned to Kilo 3/5 (K Company, 3rd Battalion 5Th Marine Regiment, 1st Marine Division). Our group was taken in the back of a 2 ½ ton truck across an open plain. "Where's our unit?" I asked the driver. He said flatly, "somewhere out there, the last I heard."

We entered a dense tree line and it looked like several hundred men were scattered throughout the clearing. It was my unit!

Within days I was reassigned to H&S Company, Motor T; and transport by another truck to Hill 69, just south of Chu Lai. On my third night in Vietnam I was on bunker watch. I never felt so alone as I did that night.

Private Kirchener was with me in the foxhole. We told each other all our secrets that night - feeling that was going to be the last night of our life - we wanted to confess all... We heard the Vietcong below the hill taunting us in English (with New York and Texas accents) "Tonight you die Marine," and "I drink your blood tonight Marine!"

I was getting shook up until Kirchener said, "Don't worry Corporal Hall, you'll be all right after you fire the first round."

Above us, on top of the hill, the weapons platoon fired several willy peter (white phosphorus) illumination mortars, that bathed the valley below in bright light. It looked like there were a billion 'black ants' (Vietcong in black pajamas), in the valley.

I told Kirchner, "It's not right!" I've only been here three days and I'm gonna die tonight!" He was right though; as soon as I fired the first round all fear left - I didn't care about life any more. I figured that I was going to take a lot of these "black ants" with me when I died.

Then suddenly I heard the artillery of Foxtrot 2/11 overhead, shells sounding like a freight train running over the top of my head. Then came the precision offshore naval gunfire - each of these shells had a killing radius of 1,000 square meters.

Seconds later, two F4C Phantoms came swooping in through the valley laying down napalm bombs right on top of "Charlie."

It was such an incredible experience! I was not as alone as I had thought. I learned again, "We are a team - we feel and we fight as one man!"

As time went on I got fed up with being scared. I grew bold, standing on a birm wall of sandbags and screaming at a sniper in the tree line, "You can't kill me...." The guys with me thought I had snapped, but actually I was growing harder and more insensitive to life. Yet in all this there was a strange compassion that I felt for the men with me; they were my brothers. They brought me their "Dear John Letters" and I would encourage them. I would tell them that it was good that they found out her unfaithfulness now - than later on after they married her. "If she's unfaithful now, she'll be unfaithful later." Then we would just have a couple of bottles of "tiger piss" (the local beer) and forget about it all.

The torture that I saw of both Marines and Charlie during this time of 2 ½ years was enough to callous my heart and attitude toward human life. At this time, our Motor T unit had the task of securing the roads around DaNang airbase. One afternoon I was riding shotgun down the Anderson Trail outside DaNang, and I heard a shot from the tree line. This was not unusual, as snipers had harassed us frequently like this. I returned fire into the tree line as we sped into the compound.

After three tours in 'Nam I was ordered to return to the States. I was done now. I just turned 21 years old and I felt like I was 60 years old.

My next duty station Stateside was MCAS El Toro, in Santa Ana, California, where I served with the Military Police for another two years. I married my high school girlfriend and we had a daughter Heidi, and a son Mark. I really enjoyed Heidi and Mark growing up, but my wife hated the Marine Corps. She finally told me to choose between the kids and the Marine Corps; because she was leaving me. I chose the kids and reluctantly left the Marine Corps after 6 ½ years of service.

## CHAPTER THREE

*Life Without The Corps*

My next 14 months were called *unemployment*. I spent most of the days filling out applications, walking to job interviews, and reading classified ads for job on the bench at a bus stop. I spent the nights worrying about our needs. It wasn't long before our cars were repossessed and food became scarce. I had resorted to taking slices of bread and cheese from my parent's home and making sandwiches for my children. I was so ashamed that I could not provide for my family. I walked in anger, frustration and bitterness with myself as a man. I was a failure.

I applied for work at a hot dog stand and told the owner that I would work for free if he would just give me a chance. I said, "after one month. If you like my work you can pay me then. He was so impressed with this offer that he hired me at $450.00 per month (1973 wages).

I had my kids with me for lunch and dinner every day! They liked the hot dogs and I was so happy that I could feed them now.

Things continued just fine until 1974 when my daughter Heidi was ready to start kindergarten. She had no clothes that fit her. She had to have nice clothes for school because she was my baby and my joy. I had to be the All-American Father - the Provider - no matter how I did it - I had to make it happen!

So, I applied for another job as a Manager Trainee for a drug store and was accepted. I was a very hard worker, always busy and diligently keeping my area of the store clean and in order.

The manager was impressed with me. When he resigned from the company and opened his building maintenance business, he asked me to join him. He didn't have to ask me twice!

We worked from about 1800 to 0600 five days a week; washing windows commercially and cleaning floors and carpets for 24-hour restaurants. Our service route grew from Santa Barbara to San Diego.

One night, the business owner and I were talking about our money problems. I was really depressed because of the lack of money in spite of my working such long hours. During out conversation the topic of robbery came up and I offered to plan a robbery.

This became an obsession with me. You see, it was the thrill of executing a carefully planned operation that became a narcotic. It drove me night and day from one robbery to another robbery.

After that first robbery I came home and left immediately to buy a car for my family. I went up to the door of a house and said; "I've come in response to your sales ad for a car." I then laid out $2,400.00 cash in $20-dollar bills on the dining room table of their house and drove away like a king in a chariot....

The money didn't satisfy me like the execution of the robbery operation did. I no longer felt like a failure (in my eyes), I felt restored as a husband and a father. I pulled up to the apartment and called to my wife, "Come on and get in, we're going shopping for groceries!" "Where did you get this car?" she asked. I told her that I got it as a bonus for my work. I don't think she ever believed me, but she stopped asking questions about it.

We went to the grocery store and I told her to take a shopping cart and start shopping from one end of the store while I took another shopping cart and started at the other end of the store. As we filled each cart we would then take another cart and fill it also. We left that store with 23 bags of groceries! The kids were thrilled with their goodies! My wife was amazed with the groceries and I was so happy at seeing their joy. The refrigerator barely closed when we loaded it up.

That night when everyone was in bed I kept getting up and going into the kitchen, opening and closing the refrigerator door, just to see those groceries - and to know that it was not just a dream.

After the second robbery I started sleeping with a gun under my pillow with a finger on the trigger. I didn't trust anyone around me.

One night before I left for "work" my wife told me "whatever you are planning to do tonight, don't do it! I don't know what it is or why, but I have a very uneasy feeling tonight." I didn't pay any attention to her. This was just another night when we would execute another carefully planned robbery.

I remember when I was in the middle of the robbery event, a feeling came over me. I felt like a runaway freight train with no brakes. was out of control. We had not even finished executing this robbery before I was beginning to plan the next robbery....

Silently, I said to myself, "Oh God, I can't stop this on my own, please get me busted tonight!" Shortly after that silent prayer, a rookie policeman was stuffing a sawed off shotgun into my neck, screaming "this is just like cops on TV."

As they led us out of the store we saw the building was surrounded by police cars with their red, yellow and blue lights flashing. We arrived at the police station and the guys in other cells told us that they had called all available units to that store location. They really wanted to capture us.

Then the police questioning began with us individually. The detective told me that my partner said that the robbery was all my idea; and he told my partner that I said the robbery was all his idea. It was their way of playing us against each other while separating us from each other in different cells. Before long, we made bail and were released.

During the next 6 months the case was prepared and we were taken to court for the trial. Before the testimony began, the witnesses, the victims in the robberies, saw us in the court hallway. They told us not to worry, that everything would be OK. When the District Attorney called each of them to testify they said that we were not the robbers; and said that whoever the robbers were, they never threatened or harmed them. In fact, the robbers had been very courteous to them.

The DA was furious, "We don't need eye witness testimony to convict on Robbery in the First Degree; we only need a similar method of operation, which we have established in this case." At the conclusion of the trial we were found guilty as charged. The sentencing hearing was then scheduled.

Before entering the courtroom on that dark day, I said good-bye to my children in the hallway. My son Mark said, "Where are you going Daddy?" I said, "Mark, when you are bad you get a spanking. When big people do bad things, they have to go to a place where bad people are." Then he said, "When are you coming home Daddy?" I told him I didn't know.

I walked through the courtroom doors to the front before the judge for sentencing. The District Attorney had told the judge, "If Mr. Hall had not made a mistake we would have never caught him. He is an extremely dangerous man." The judge looked down at me and said, "I sentence you to what the law prescribes for these crimes: 9 sentences of 5 years to life to be run consecutively. We never want to see you on the streets again!"

I was so overwhelmed that I became dizzy and fell into a chair. The Marshall quickly rushed to me and grabbed my arms, pushing me through the back door of the court into the cages - what they called "the tank." I was now a "fish," a brand new inmate in the California Department of Corrections; and my name was changed to B-63934.

I was sent to the Inmate Reception Center in Chino, California where they would determine which prison I would be permanently housed in. Six months later I was transferred to Folsom Prison in

Repressa, California. They had each of us put on white coveralls, shackled our hands and legs with chains; then chained us to the seat in the bus so we couldn't escape in the event of an accident with the bus.

The ride was long; 7 hours long. Looking at the cars driving past crushed me; seeing the families in the cars and knowing my family had been dissolved, like cream in a cup of coffee. I was empty, bitter and dying inside. I was a broken man.

From the road I could see this place that looked like Frankenstein's Castle, a dungeon, such a wicked place of hopelessness. It's nickname "the warehouse," fit its character well. This prison was carved out of a rock.

We entered through a series of three gates, each one closing behind the bus, and each one emphasizing the depth of my despair. As I was led past the officer outside the bus, he looked at my manila file jacket and saw my sentence of 9 consecutive life terms, and said, "What are you doing here, son? You're so young!"

I didn't say anything. Inside I moaned, "I want to get out of here and go home and be with my kids, hear their laughter again, feel their little arms around my neck, hear their precious little giggles..."

## CHAPTER FOUR

## *DEAD MAN . . . WALKING*

They separated us "lifers" from the convicts with 10 to 25-year sentences; and led us to Block 4A. In the cell that day I realized that this would be my world now. It was a small world. I walked 5 steps one way and 3 steps the other way. I was going to die an empty old man in this hole. The first time we were lead out of our separate cells I remember the guard saying dead men walking. I was to hear this phrase repeated many more times. Each time I heard it, I became more hollow, empty and dead inside.

Overhead walkways were covered in barbed wire and criss-crossed the ceiling over us. Guards walked constantly with shotguns ready to shoot us at the least provocation. We were isolated from the rest of the prison population, ate alone, showered alone, and walked the yard alone.

The first time in the shower area and old man whispered in my ear, "if you drop the soap sonny, just let it lay there...." I got his drift about not bending over and thought to myself, "These guys are really sick!" One night in my cell I began thinking about my life. I thought, "I know I'm going to die here one day," and then another thought came to me. "What are you waiting for, just kill yourself now." We had no belts or anything to hang our self with, so if a lifer wanted to kill himself he just grabbed the cell bars and beat his head into the bars, until they bled to death; nobody cared.

I was getting ready to do this when a series of questions and answers began floating in and out of my mind. "Remember when you were 7 years old in Sunday School and you heard a voice behind you say, "One day you will preach My Gospel," and you turned around and no one was there?

Remember as a teenager when this happened again on the way home from school in the afternoon?

Remember in Vietnam all the times you said you wanted to be a Christian, because of fear, and all the times you made excuses delaying your decision to give me your life?

God began to show me who I really was. I was disgusting! I was not the All-American husband and father, or smart guy. I was a loser and a fool that was heading for hell on a greased pole!

I cried, "Oh God is this why I was born, to die in a place like this? I'm sorry for what I did and I know I'm going to spend the rest of my life in here, but I don't want to die this way; with fear and emptiness in my heart."

Then God said "give Me your life." "But, I don't have a life to give You, I'm a dead man walking. Oh God, whatever I have, and here's my breath; I just want peace in my heart. Please, if You are for real, God please do something!"
I'm sure this must have been the sloppiest sinner's prayer ever prayed; but that night, in that hour, Jesus Christ received my sin-sick life and put me to sleep.

Something radical had happened because when I woke up in the morning everything seemed to be bright! The emptiness and hopeless feeling were gone. I didn't want anything anymore. I wanted to give everything away. I remember saying, "Oh Jesus, You, came out of the Bible and into my life, You truly are for real." I was so happy that I started skipping in the yard that day. The guards saw my happiness and accused me of being high on "pruno" (jailhouse whiskey), or sniffing socks soaked in acetone. I just told them that "I got Jesus last night."

The circumstances around me were all the same, but my view of those circumstances was completely new! It did not matter to me where I was or what was going on with me. He was with me, and His presence made my cell like the Hilton Hotel and the food I ate was like a royal banquet. Everything became different and I felt like somehow Jesus had lifted me above all the despair and loneliness I had felt.

Jesus was, and is all I really need.

You will never know that Jesus is all you need - until Jesus is all you have.

That day I heard a man named Oral Roberts speaking on the radio and all I could remember was a partial address: Oral Roberts, Tulsa, Oklahoma. So I wrote a letter to him asking him for a Bible. In 3 days I received my Bible, which was a real miracle. I read my new Bible day and night, I couldn't get enough. I was full of questions like a little boy. It was so wonderful. I asked Jesus to never let this joy end, because I wanted it to last forever. I had been happy before but it had always ended, so I told Jesus, "I don't want to ever lose this joy I have with You."

I remember Him saying to me, "Billy, remember these three things and you will never lose your joy: First: <u>Remember Who I Am.</u> I am God, the only True and Living God. I will never change and I will never leave you. I will never give up on you. I understand and know you better than you know yourself. I love you with an everlasting and unchangeable love. My ultimate goal is to make you like Myself. This is Who I Am, I am on your side. Second: <u>Remember Who You Are In Me.</u> You are My son and My friend when you obey My commands and walk with Me. All that I have is yours. All the resources of heaven are at your call. I have given you My Word, the Bible, to read, to help you know who you are in Me, and all that I have for you. Holy Spirit is in you to Guide you. He will teach you and help you do the right things. Heaven knows you as My very own son. Third: <u>Remember Where You Are Going.</u> This world is not your home. Your home is Heaven and you will live forever in Heaven with Me. No more tears, frustration, fighting with the devil, or painful suffering. Every day, you are one day closer to coming home than you were the previous day."

As He spoke to me of His great love I began to expect great things to happen. Later that week, a guard came to my cell and said they were transferring me to another prison further up north to a city named Susanville. The next two weeks passed quickly and soon I was packed and on my way. This time the bus ride was even longer than the first one. I began to think about my family again. I missed my son and daughter so much. What were they doing now? Who is playing with them, feeling their loving arms and laughing with them? I thought, "God, will You ever put these broken pieces back together again?"

That is when God promised to give me a wife. Somewhat confused I asked Him, "What will I do with a wife in prison? I mean Lord, I'm going to spend the rest of my life in prison. My wife and my children are gone; their husband and father is as good as dead. They will have an entirely different life now without me; and You're talking about *another* wife for me? That doesn't make sense."

As we pulled into the yard at Susanville I noticed it looked more like a school than a prison. Upon arrival, my record was reviewed by the warden's staff and it was recommended that I be assigned as a teacher's aid in a place they called the Vocational Skill Center. The convicts who worked in the admin area also saw my file and the word spread quickly about my crime and my jacket. Your "jacket" is the term to describe your behavior, character, and the way you've acted since you were in prison. Your jacket can earn you a "rep," reputation of respect on the yard - or earn you a "target on your back," if you are a child molester, rapist, or a cop.

My jacket described me as a loner, with no prison gang affiliation, no prior convictions and a virtual new kid on the block. I was so involved with Jesus, reading His Word, and talking and listening to Him in my heart, that I didn't pay attention to what was going on around me. For those first few months I just did what I felt was natural to me. I knew that I wanted to do something useful with the rest of my life, even though I was in prison. So, when I was given the opportunity to attend the evening college classes in the prison, I jumped at the chance!

My heart had been totally changed! I began treating everyone the same, regardless of their race or gang affiliation. When a person needed help I gladly spent time helping them with their homework assignments. When they offered to pay me back with packs or cartons of cigarettes (jail house currency), I said, "I don't smoke." If they offered drugs, I said "I don't use drugs." When they offered to pay in other ways I said, "I don't need or want anything. I just enjoy doing something to help you. Their universal response was, "Why? What's in this for you?" I told them, "nothing. I guess I've received so much from Jesus already, that I have to give some of it away or I'll burst." The convicts could not understand this attitude, so I invited them to my "hooch," where I slept; where I took out my Bible and read to them. Then I would explain what those verses meant to me. Often, they would get nervous after a while and leave. But I know that God used His Word to impact their lives. Some of them just said I was weird, but they came back to me again later to talk about stuff.

    The guards would say, "Hall is a convict but he's not a convict, I don't know how to describe him." God was with me in the middle of this tension between convicts and guards; and caused me to have favor with both convicts and guards. I wasn't afraid of death like the others, so threats didn't move me. In fact, I looked forward to my death, because the Bible said that this was the way I could enjoy being face to face with Jesus forever. I look back on these years and see myself "unknowingly" as Daniel in the lion's den, walking among the lions - yet, like Daniel, I was untouched.

Oh, the Amazing Love of Jesus is a wonder to me.

As I read my Bible more and more I began to understand it and I saw things that I never realized before. It started to make sense to me. There was another unique lesson I learned about scripture - it was continually alive - and actively showing me something new as I read it. I often thought to myself, "Oh Billy, you don't know anything!" Every time I thought I had exhausted the possibilities of "meaning" in a verse, God showed me another interesting thought.

God's Word is so very deep. It's like a lake that is deep enough so that the most intelligent student could dive in and never touch the bottom of the lake; yet it's shallow enough for a little new kid like me to step in slowly, with a sense of awe and wonder.

One afternoon as I was reading my Bible I became curious about fasting. I read about the principles of fasting, and the incredible power that came upon the lives of people in the Bible who fasted. I decided to fast the next day.

Some of the convicts came and asked me why I wasn't eating. I told them it was because I wasn't hungry ('cause I didn't want them to know I was fasting, because the Bible said that we should do this in secret). This went on for a few days. On the third day, as I was between sleeping and awake, I saw a beautiful vision on the wall in front of my rack. There was a man kneeling down in front of a large white rock in a garden. He was looking at the sky and I saw white writing appear across the wall:
"Love, patient woe;
Love meeting no response;
Yet still remaining love."

I said, "Oh God, I see, this is Your love for me. How You loved me when I didn't love You! Your Love doesn't depend on me, it depends on You, and You are Jesus Christ the same yesterday, today and forever. Oh I want to love others just like You do." He promised me then and there that He would teach me to love His way.

One of the first guys I met in Susanville was a short burley fellow named Leon. He was nearly as broad as he was tall. Leon was with me a lot, or at least looking for me. I thought it was because he just wanted to talk, but one day I found out what was really on his mind. While we were walking to the weight lifting area, he put his arm around my neck and said, "Billy, you don't know what you do to me!"

At first, I felt like I was going to vomit, and then I became really angry. I grabbed his arm and then ripped it away yelling, "knock it off Leon, and get on your knees!!"

Suddenly, I noticed that several convicts were staring at us, and Leon was stunned. I dropped to my knees and heard God say, "Tell Leon that I'm going to do a miracle for him to prove Who I am."

I said, "Leon, God says He wants you to ask for a miracle and He will do it, what is your miracle?"

Leon started crying like a little baby and said, "I want to see my momma. She is old and I'm afraid that she will die before I ever get out of here. I want to see her before she dies."

I took hold of his enormous hands and began to pray, "God, You said that You would do this miracle and we have asked You just as You told us to. Thank You God for doing this miracle in Leon's life.

As we got up I noticed a small crowd had gathered, gazing in wonder at this enormous black man and this skinny little white boy talking so boldly to him. This is not a common sight in a prison system filled with hatred, racism, murder, rape, and all manner of perversion.

Leon mocked me and my prayer in the days and weeks that followed this event. "I'm still here Billy, maybe your God can't hear you, maybe you're just a liar, or maybe God hates black people. I fought back the anger and tried to ignore his mocking.

It was several months later as I was just beginning to cross the football size prison yard, that I heard a man scream "Billyyyyyyy!!" I looked across the yard and many convicts were standing around the edge of the yard, the guards were leaning out of their gun towers with their rifles as Leon was running toward me - and I was running toward him. Everyone else just saw a big black man and a little white boy running at each other; the blood was going to fly!

We met near the center of the yard and Leon fell on his knees weeping. "The Warden, Billy, he called me to his office just a few minutes ago and said he was sending me home in just 10 days!" I replied, "See Leon, don't you ever forget what God just did for you. Give Him your life and serve Him." Sobbing with joy, he said, "Oh Billy, I'll never forget this."

Leon was a changed man and my faith had grown to a new level. I was learning to love others and obey God instead of trying to understand Him.

As a teacher's aide in the drafting class it was my responsibility to issue paper and tools to the convicts attending the drafting class. One day a fellow named Jesse asked for more paper than the instructor allowed. I refused and as I was turning away from him he hit me in the jaw and I fell down. As I got up, I saw the whole class standing ready to start fighting. Racial tension was always ready to explode at the slightest provocation. I said, "It's all right everybody, just cool it." Inside, I was raging, "God help me not to lose my testimony, help me keep my mouth shut and get rid of this anger."

After the class, we all went to the mess hall for the evening meal. I sat alone because I felt isolated and upset. Jesse came to my table, got down on his knees and asked me to forgive him. I was very uncomfortable with this, but I told him it was OK and asked him to please just leave me alone. After I finished eating I went outside, walked and ran around the yard until the anger was out of my head. One of the leaders in the black prison gang came up to me and walked alongside me. He asked me if Jesse had talked with me. I said yes. "Well, what did you tell him Billy?" I said I had forgiven him and that it was OK. He said, "You just saved Jesse's life. Tonight, we were going to kill him for what he did to you." He continued, "Billy, you don't realize it, but you've been adding up favors from all over the yard here with the convicts. From now on, wherever you go in the system, no one will ever touch a hair of your head without answering to the rest of us.

I had no idea this was going on. I was just doing what I wanted to do - sharing the overflowing abundance of what God was filling me with - His love!

# CHAPTER FIVE

## *The Son Has Set You Free*

Everyone was watching me. The guards were watching to see if they could catch me doing something wrong and prove me to be a liar instead of a Christian. Some of the convicts were watching me to see if there were any weaknesses they could exploit in me. One thing that I was learning very well was that my life was constantly under a microscope.

After the first year in prison my previous life experience seemed like a dream. I felt like I had never been outside of prison and that I had always lived here. Prison had become the only real world to me. I had only one Christian brother on the other side of the prison that I was only able to see infrequently.

In time, my job assignment was changed to "Personnel Assignment Clerk." I typed the duty rosters for the guards. They offered to buy me hamburgers and steak sandwiches to obtain favors but I refused. I refused favors from the convicts on the yard as well as the prison staff; and this had made me an untouchable. I felt this might obligate me to them, and I refused to be obligated to anyone but Jesus.

I was given a key that would unlock the gate to the office where I worked at any time; I had access to this office 24 hours a day. This was really great for my personal study time and quiet time with God.

The most memorable event happened after I had been in prison for 2 ½ years. I was walking across the yard one afternoon and a voice came over the loudspeaker and said "B-63934 report to the warden's office." I was surprised at this, not knowing why the Warden would want to see me. When I walked into his office I saw that he was sitting with two members of the Parole Board. They reviewed my record and mocked my Christian experience and insulted me. This seemed to me like an attempt to get me to lose my temper, do something violent, so they could punish me. I gripped the arm of the chair so hard that if came off in my hand. Then they became quiet, then said "B-63934, we are sending you home in 6 months." I was shocked and speechless. I left the room with tears running down my cheek. The convicts outside the room were wondering what happened inside the room that made me cry, but I couldn't even talk.

I had no desire to get out of prison. I was so happy with my Jesus and the Holy Spirit. I said, "Why God, are You letting me out?" When I regained my composure, I told the guys I was being sent home in 6 months. It was truly a miracle - an absolute miracle!

The next day, the Chairman of the Parole Board revoked my release date, saying that the Board could not legally release me unless the Governor approved and signed off on the release date. My release date was sent to the Governor's Office where it was approved, and 4 months later I was a free man.

When I walked through the very last gate, Officer Hallinan said, "You'll be back, they all come back and you are no different." But when I walked through that gate I felt as if the ground opened up and I had just stepped out of a grave - it was a miracle!

There were two vaguely familiar men waiting for me outside in the parking lot. I thought I had seen them before in prison. They said, "We came for you Billy. We appreciate what you did for our people in prison and want to offer you a job as a legal and financial advisor. They took me to their car and began the long drive home, some 750 miles. As we went down the mountainside I asked them to stop. I got out and walked up the mountainside a short distance and sat down by a running stream alone - I started to cry. I just couldn't believe that I was outside those walls.

At a nearby store I went in to buy some new clothes. When I came out with them they wanted to see what I bought. I showed them my new blue shirt and blue jeans (the same clothes as my prison clothes). They asked, "Why did you buy those clothes?" (pointing out the similarity of my old prison clothes). I was surprised. Out of all the clothes in that store, what did I choose but those same old clothes that I had worn in prison. I was amazed at how much my mind had been conditioned by my prison surroundings.

When we arrived in Los Angeles they gave me the car, $500.00 in cash, and said if I needed more money to call them and they would give me whatever I needed. "Take a couple of weeks and think about it Billy. You can name your price," I felt confused. I knew it was wrong to "throw-in" with them, yet I also knew that I would have a real tough time finding work as an ex-convict. I really struggled during those days.

After two weeks, I called them and asked them to meet me at a local restraint. I gave them back the car and said the only way they could pay me for what I had done was to give their life to Jesus. They were very surprised. I said, "For almost three years I lived three lives simultaneously; the life of the convict to stay alive, the life for the guard to keep from catching another beef (an additional prison sentence), and the life of a Christian. I'm gonna simply life one life now. The life of a Christian." I said, "Good-bye."

I ten bought a 1960 VW Bug and it became my house. I got a bucket, a pole, and a squeegee, and began going to gas stations offering to wash windows for $10 or $15. I used the money from washing windows for gasoline, bread and bologna and cheese for my meals. I was too ashamed to ask my parent's permission to live with them. Instead, I told them I was staying somewhere else. I gave their address to my parole officer as my place of residence and he met me there each month to check on me and my behavior. I remember him telling me many times that I was the only one in his entire caseload that called him to remind him of our appointment.

After only a few months I started a part-time job I got from an employment agency owned by a friend of my dad's (who gave me a 'pass' on my ex-convict status). My job as a clerk was to post additions and subtractions from individual inventory cards for a plumbing specialty company. I was making $2.25 per hour and I felt like I was rich! I thought, "Now I'll be able to get a small apartment to live in." At this new job I was always the first one to work, waiting for someone to arrive and open the door in the morning. In the evening everyone was gone except the president and me, and he had to order me to leave. I was so excited about this job.

After a few months, the president came up to me and asked if I knew how to do bookkeeping. Under my breath I said, in Jesus' name by faith, "Yes, I do!" "I can do that." (I can do all things through Christ Jesus). He said He was firing the bookkeeper and wanted me to begin this position first thing Monday morning. All weekend I was praying. "Jesus, You are the Best Bookkeeper. You know all about bookkeeping and You can teach me all I need to know."

That Monday morning as I began looking through the past records and the way the other bookkeeper had done her work, the Holy Spirit began to help me learn. He suggested that I call the CPA for the company and invite him to have lunch with me. So, I did! I told him that I was the new bookkeeper and I wanted to know how he would like me to prepare the bookkeeping records for him; so, he would have an easier time auditing at the end of the year. The CPA was thrilled that I wanted to help him do his work. I became his student and we became very good friends.

As things progressed the president began to place more and more responsibility on me until I became the Corporate Controller in charge of Employment Benefit Plans, Pension Plan Administration, Personnel, and the Commercial Insurance Plan for our company. My salary for this 3-year period of employment went from $2.25 per hour to $4,500.00 per month! The president approved a loan for me of $26,000 as a down payment on a 3 bedroom and 2 bath home in a beautiful area of Pasadena, California.

My life was really moving fast now! I was looking for a church home and everywhere I went to share my testimony, people were anxious to hear what God had done - but they could not forget about my past. I was still often seen as a convict, untouchable by them and definitely not a part of their family.

About a year after I was released from prison I pulled into a gas station for gas. When I paid for the gas at the booth, I slipped a Gospel Tract with my payment to the cashier. When the cashier saw the Gospel Tract she smiled and so I said, "With a smile like that you must be a Christian." She said that she was and asked what church I attended. I said I was looking for a church and then she invited me to her church on that Sunday. She said, "You'll love my Pastor, his name is Michael Neville." I picked her and her mom up on Sunday and together we went to the wonderful church in Maywood, California. Walking in the door I was overwhelmed with the sense of genuine love. I felt as though I had finally come home. A man named Robert Bloom was teaching Sunday School that day. After class I introduced myself and hugged him as a brother in Christ. I felt as though we had always been brothers and friends. This was to be my spiritual home, my local church community, in the beautiful city of Maywood, California.

Not long after this I was impressed by God to enroll in Law School. At first this seemed like everything else that God had ever put on my heart to do; it initially made no sense to me. I thought, "Here I am, an ex-convict on parole for the rest of my life, and God wants <u>me</u> to go to law school." My applications were rejected by the schools as soon as they obtained my background report. Finally, as I was speaking with the Registrar of the Law School I came right out and flatly told him, "Sir, I'm an ex-felon and I've been out of prison for about 2 ½ years." He got up from his chair and went to close the door, so we could have some privacy. Then, leaning forward respectfully, he asked "Please tell me how you came to be in prison and what has happened in your life since then."

That was all the opening I needed. I shared my testimony with him, telling him all that Jesus has done for me. When I finished He said, "It would be a pleasure to have you in my law school. I plan to take a personal interest in your success." That settled it.

Every night I drove across town to the campus where classes began at 6:00pm until 9:30 pm. All the students were working full-time and commuting to school at night. Even the law professors were working full-time during the day in their own law practices.

Our first class started with about 60 students. By the end of that first year there were only 15 of us left. By the end of the third year there were only 4 of us left from the original 60 students; me and my study partner Eric, and two girls who were also study partners. The classes were extremely demanding. We briefed 30 to 45 cases per class each night (3 classes). We had to know all the pertinent facts of each case, be prepared to argue both sides of each case, and give a conclusion as to what the judge would probably rule on each of the legal issues of each case. We never knew which case the professor would call us to recite. I can hear him like it was yesterday: "Mr. Hall, stand and give us the facts of the Nemier Case." I would then stand up and recite the facts of the case; the issue, the rule of law, the arguments for and against, and the conclusion.

One night a fellow student was recoting the facts of a criminal law case of grand theft auto. In his conclusion, he casually said, "this guy will only do 2 or 3 years in prison for this crime, it will be easy for him." I immediately spoke up and asked him, "how would you like to go down to the county jail with me for a day, stay in lock up for 24 hours, and see how easy that would be for you!"

Everyone grew very silent so the professor called a quick break and we all went out into the hallway. My study partner Eric came to me and said, "Billy, you talked like you have been in prison." I have Eric," I said, "and it's no easy time. Young guys like car thieves, with no prior record, go to prison and get raped, tortured, and come out mean, bitter, cold and much better educated about committing other crimes. The 'Joint' is virtually a Criminal University." We never talked about my prison experience again.

# CHAPTER SIX

*Called To Serve*

As I continued learning more about accounting, pension plan administration, and employee benefit plan administration; I decided to start an accounting practice in my home. I gathered a group of 12 different clients from businesses like gas stations, leather specialty stores, luggage repair, auto body repair, and industrial manufacturing businesses.

My classes in law school, work as a controller, and accounting business, all tied together giving me a unique community in which to evangelize. Holy Spirit was constantly giving me opportunities to pray for people, share the compassion of Jesus with them and invite them to church. I was so happy being with so many different people and lifestyles, from South Central Los Angeles, Watts, San Fernando Valley, Westwood Village, Beverly Hills, and even having dinner with my client and Jaclyn Smith one evening.

One really exciting part of my life was the singles Home Bible Study Group we called "Sheepfold," that I was a part of in those years. So many people were coming to Jesus and growing up in their relationship with Him. It was like living with walking and talking miracles - every one of them were living miracles that continued to unfold in each meeting. Saturday afternoon was out meeting time.

Eventually, I was asked to be an assistant Home Bible Study Leader. I remember my very first sermon. I was so nervous. I had spent two weeks preparing the sermon. It was 10 pages long! As we were singing and praising God, I felt God saying, "I don't want you to preach that message tonight." Silently I said, "Oh no God, don't do this to me. They're going to ask me to share the message after this song, and without this message I have nothing to share." He said, "I will give you the message to share." I heard this crystal clear!

As I stood behind the pulpit, the Lord said to me, "Turn to Proverbs Chapter 31." And I said, "Turn to Proverbs Chapter 31." And that is all I remember from that very first sermon. What God told me, I repeated; and so He led us through this chapter, verse by verse. At the end I prayed and gave the invitation to those who wanted to receive

Jesus as their Lord and Savior. After the meeting, some people came up to me and explained to me how God had uniquely touched them, convicted them, and helped them to understand this message. I was so happy for them and also happy that this stressful experience was past me now. Through many years, I've looked back on this experience several times; and been reminded as to how God wants me to be when I step into His pulpit - waiting for His approval of the sermon before I open my mouth.

Staying holy was not easy for me during those difficult years. I remembered God's promise to me of a wife and partner in ministry, but five long and hard years had come and gone without any change whatsoever. I began to be discouraged, and finally one day I said, "God, just let me be like the apostle Paul; I guess I really don't need a wife. I have You and I'm really happy with just You."

God knew my heart and I must confess that I really did want a wife. I was lonely. I missed my children and I didn't want to go home at night because it was such a lonely place to be. God began to tell me more about my wife He had promised to me.

She was married before, just like me, but her husband died. She was almost as tall as me. She had experienced a very difficult life and she had two children; a girl and a boy, the girl being the oldest. As He told me about her life, I began to pray for her and the children; instead of for myself. When I felt lonely, I prayed for her wherever she was, that she would not experience loneliness.

One night as I was lying in bed, I started to cry and I asked God, "Please don't ever let me forget how lonely I feel tonight; so I will always appreciate the woman You have for me."

Some of the ladies in the church had shown an interest in me. I was also interested in them as well. So, I asked God how, would I be able to know which one was the right one. He said, "Ask Me for a sign." I didn't know how so I asked Him to give me a sign. So, He told me: "<u>First</u>, you will not be physically attracted to each other, initially. Your primary attraction will be spiritual.
<u>Second,</u> she must answer <u>Yes</u> to each of these questions: Will you spill your blood for Jesus? Then ask her: If I was place before you to be tortured and soldiers asked you will you choose Jesus instead of me, and let them torture and kill me?

For twelve years no one was willing to spill their blood for Jesus, and all of them kept their distance from me after this!

Growing up in the Maywood congregation was an exciting experience for me. There was never a routine service. I was introduced to the spiritual language of tongues in the first service, during the worship and praise time. Although it seemed a little weird as first but soon there was a sense of calm that made me feel that this would be alright. "I'll just set this experience on the shelf and God will help me understand this later on." Like so many amazing spiritual truths I learned during those years, this was forming character in me and moving me into the unique destiny God had for my life.

Sometimes it seems as Christians we stumble into destiny by just doing what the Bible says to do: "Be faithful in the little things; (Daily Prayer, Bible Study, Church attendance and participation). These little things are big things in God's eyes.

I remember when Pastor Neville called Pastor Johnny and Patti Dorris to the front of the church and announced that we were sending them to Ontario to start a new church. The church did not have the money to do this, so Pastor Neville simply said: "We're all going to do our part and God will give us the money we need - let's give to God." The music played, we sang, we each did our part, and God made a way where there seemed to be no way as each one of us gave what we had.

    After Pastor John and Patti went, others went also, all my friends were leaving it seemed. I sensed there was something that God wanted to do with my life but I didn't know what it was. I felt like I was in the "spiritual bleachers" and everyone else was on the "spiritual battlefield." I became determined to find out what God's plan for my life was! I vowed to God that day in early November 1980, that I would not eat anything until He spoke to me, and told me what ministry He had called me to engage in.

    Toward the second week of fasting, I was alone in the computer room at my job entering financial information. Suddenly I felt dizzy, and a breeze seemed to be blowing in the room. Questions and answers began penetrating my mind rapidly, like machine gun fire. "Did you ever wonder why you survived all the killing in Vietnam - Do you know what it is like to live in a communist

country? Did you ever wonder why you passed all those years in prison - Do you know what it's like to be in a communist prison?" Then His word came, crystal clear: "I have called you to the communist nations; I am giving you East Germany, Poland, Hungary, Yugoslavia, Czechoslovakia, Romania, Bulgaria, Russia, China, and Ethiopia. These are your babies; pray for them as a father prays for his children.
I will break the back of Communism and the world will know that I the Lord God have done this work. I will take you there <u>without</u> money from your church but <u>with</u> the prayers of your church."

I was delirious, between sleep and being awake. It seemed so big, so frightening, and so exciting. It was Friday and we had church that night. Excitedly, I told Pastor Neville about this new revelation I had received from God. He said that our church had no experience in communist countries, and that we always sent financial support to those we sent out to ministry. If God is in this, He will put it together! I will pray with you and we will let God put this whole thing together." While some mocked and made fun of me, Pastor Neville believed God with me and prayed.

In obedience to God's direction, I began to give my business clients away to accountants that I knew, and I finished my law school education. I was preparing to leave on a moment's notice. Now, I had my "Mission Assignment," and I was locked and loaded! I had an intense focus to pour my energy into and my prayer life became more intense. As a result of this growing passion God began to do special things for me in my prayer life. He would wake me up in the middle of the night to pray. I did not know what to pray for so I praised Him singing and loving Him until I fell asleep.

One night as I was drifting between sleep and consciousness, I fell into a trance and woke up lying on a bench in a park. It was evening and I could feel the heavy mist as I looked at the stone walls surrounding this large park. I heard the sound of what seemed to be soldiers marching, I saw them. They were all wearing swastika arm bands. A voice told me, "You are in East Germany now, Billy." I felt fear and terror like I had never known before. The sense of hopelessness and oppression nearly suffocated me. I really felt a deep evil presence. After a while, I woke up to discover that it was only a dream. I felt the awe and wonder of knowing that God had made this so real to me. I could actually feel a little of what these precious souls of East Germany were feeling. I sensed a greater power and passion growing in my prayer life.

A few months later, I was awakened during the night with another vision. This time, an older woman was holding a telephone to her ear and asking me to pray for her husband. He was in trouble and her voice sounded so desperate. A voice told me that she was Russian, and then I woke up. I rolled out of bed and said, "Lord, I promise to pray and fast until this lady gets her victory and her husband is set free." I did not know the details of the problem! I didn't care about them. I just wanted to help this desperate woman and her husband.

Three days after this, I was awakened again to another vision in the middle of the night. This time the older lady was on the telephone again with me. I saw her husband, an older man, sitting next to her as she spoke to me. "Billy, thank you for praying for us. Everything is all right now. Thank you for praying for us." I was so excited when I woke up. God promised me that I would meet this woman and her husband one day. They would recognize me and I would recognize them.

Another night as I was praying and falling asleep, I found myself in a basement somewhere. I was in a corner and the place was cold and damp. A voice told me this was in Bulgaria. There were lots of people there; men, women, and children all huddled together. Suddenly, a loud voice commanded them to stand up. The soldiers began firing and their bodies flew like rag dolls to the floor. The murderer's dug a deep hole and threw their bodies in and covered them up with dirt. Then they placed a metal cover on top of the hole, like a heavy manhole cover. I came and knelt by the cover and saw a writing on it that said: "The Bulgarian 13." I kissed that cold metal cover and cried, and cried, and cried.... when I woke up in the morning I was still crying out to God.

Soon after this I met a Chinese lady through a mutual friend who was a tutor for the language of Mandarin Chinese. I hired her to be my tutor. Ahn Sue was a great teacher. In each session she would teach me basics and she also would include a verse of scripture. She taught me to speak Mandarin the same way I learned to speak English; like a little child. Every Saturday afternoon we had 2 to 3 hours together, reading, writing, and speaking Mandarin.

After about 6 months of instruction, I was invited by an organization, The English Language Institute in China, (ELIC) to apply for a position as a "Foreign Expert" in teaching English in China. I was so excited. I thought, "this <u>must</u> be the door of opportunity I've been waiting two years for." I was asked what courses I wanted to teach and the textbooks I wanted to use. I agreed to teach two classes; one on history, and one on personal relationships. The textbook for history would be the Old Testament of the Bible, and the textbook for personal relationships would be the New Testament of the Bible. My "textbook" was accepted. I felt this was a certain sign that this was the will of God.

I went to my Pastor to see what he thought about this opportunity. He shared with me the insight of seeking the <u>perfect</u> will of God for my life; not simply the will of God. He prayed with me during the week I was given to make a decision. At the end of the week I was still excited about this opportunity; but my Pastor was not comfortable about it. He has always given me the freedom to choose the will of God for my life, however, I had asked God to always confirm His will for me through the heart of my Pastor; the one He had made responsible over my spiritual life. Since Pastor Neville was not comfortable with this opportunity I decided to withdraw my application.

1982 came and went with this new lesson in spiritual maturity; distinguishing between the <u>permissive</u> and the <u>perfect</u> will of God for my life. It's easy to be satisfied with second best, the permissive will of God; but I wanted to please my Commander Jesus, and I could only do this by choosing His perfect will for my life.

One Thursday morning I got a phone call from a friend named David Riggs. David was a special friend to me in the early years at Maywood. He and his wife Lauri had befriended me. David had worked as a gardener and tree trimmer when he was younger and so had I. We talked about all these things in my life a lot. David and Lauri had been sent to Sun Valley to start a new church. He was a man of passion and zeal that was contagious to those around him. On this Thursday morning he began to tell me about a dream that his wife Lauri had the night before.

*He said that she was walking in a large and wide river bed. There were many large rocks and stones and the way was very hot and dry and difficult for her. He was also walking along the dry river bed watching her struggle. Suddenly, I appeared near to her and David called to me and asked me to walk with her for a while and help her through this dry and difficult walk. I came and then began walking with her and then she woke up.*

He asked me for my interpretation of the dream. I told him that I felt the dream was symbolic of his church. He was seen as the head of the church and Lauri was seen as the church; I was simply myself. David felt that God was asking me to help him and Lauri to build this new church. We both shared this with Pastor Neville and he had the same interpretation of the dream. He said it was up to me if I would leave Maywood and help David in Sun Valley. So I went to Sun Valley.

It was a difficult time for us in the Sun Valley church. Many people were coming to Christ but they were not remaining in the church. There were only about 15 of us back then. The street outreaches were pretty exciting, in the mall parking lots, and shopping centers. We split up into three teams to reach three different areas of the city at the same time.

One night when I was preaching in a K-Mart Parking Lot God did a special wonder for one of our new converts. As I was walking back and forth in the lot, fours cars intentionally drove from all directions to box me in. I climbed over their bumper and continued to preach. One man came running up behind me with a club ready to hit me. She told us later that she saw this man running with a club to hit me and then the man stopped suddenly like something or someone was holding him back, he just stood still. We believed that she had seen God's invisible angels fighting on our behalf, protecting us from unknown danger.

On another outreach, we went to a huge movie theater complex. The Movie Star Wars was being shown for the first time. I told the team to stand in line with at least 10 to 15 people between each team member. The line was all around the building and I knew the people would be standing there a long time. This would be a captive audience. After we were in the line for a while we began talking with the people in front and behind us. Then two of the men from the church began preaching the Gospel across the street from the parking lot, and we encouraged them saying Amen! By the time the line went into the theater everyone had heard the Gospel and our personal testimony of how we received Christ as our Lord and Savior.

As I was walking across the parking lot later that night, a young man came up to me and asked me how he could be saved. I led him in the sinner's prayer and gave him my address and we exchanged telephone numbers. I counted this outreach a success even if it was just for this one person.

Our little 220 square foot building was filling up again with new converts, but the finances were not enough for all the bills. Our rent for the church building was past due, and without a miracle, the landlord told us he was going to padlock the doo while bringing a prodigal son back.

I remember praying with David on a Saturday morning, with our faces pressed against the wall. I cried, "God, please do something! Show us what we must do. We are desperate and depending on You. Don't let the devil have this victory!" Our desperate prayer continued that morning until early afternoon. David went back to his house and I went back to mine. That afternoon David called me excitedly sharing this incredible testimony.

A backslidden brother from the church had called him and asked him to come over to his house and pray for him. David went and prayed, leading him back to the Lord. As David was leaving, the man called to him and said, "Oh Pastor David, here I want to give you my back tithes!" This amounted to several hundred dollars. God had met our need in this powerful way while bringing a prodigal son back home at the same time! He is so wonderful!

*large rocks and stones and the way was very hot and dry and difficult for her. He was also walking along the dry river bed watching her struggle. Suddenly, I appeared near to her and David called to me and asked me to walk with her for a while and help her through this dry and difficult walk. I came and then began walking with her and then she woke up.*

He asked me for my interpretation of the dream. I told him that I felt the dream was symbolic of his church. He was seen as the head of the church and Lauri was seen as the church; I was simply myself. David felt that God was asking me to help him and Lauri to build this new church. We both shared this with Pastor Neville and he had the same interpretation of the dream. He said it was up to me if I would leave Maywood and help David in Sun Valley. So I went to Sun Valley.

It was a difficult time for us in the Sun Valley church. Many people were coming to Christ but they were not remaining in the church. There were only about 15 of us back then. The street outreaches were pretty exciting, in the mall parking lots, and shopping centers. We split up into three teams to reach three different areas of the city at the same time.

One night when I was preaching in a K-Mart Parking Lot God did a special wonder for one of our new converts. As I was walking back and forth in the lot, fours cars intentionally drove from all directions to box me in. I climbed over their bumper and continued to preach. One man came running up behind me with a club ready to hit me. She told us later that she saw this man running with a club to hit me and then the man stopped suddenly like something or someone was holding him back, he just stood still. We believed that she had seen God's invisible angels fighting on our behalf, protecting us from unknown danger.

On another outreach, we went to a huge movie theater complex. The Movie Star Wars was being shown for the first time. I told the team to stand in line with at least 10 to 15 people between each team member. The line was all around the building and I knew the people would be standing there a long time. This would be a captive audience. After we were in the line for a while we began talking with the people in front and behind us. Then two of the men from the church began preaching the Gospel across the street from the parking lot, and we encouraged them saying Amen! By the time the line went into the theater everyone

# CHAPTER SEVEN

*Out Of My Tree*

Fund raising involves some really unique things. We had a chance to raise $600.00 for the church by cutting down a huge walnut tree for one the evangelists of our Fellowship. David would be on the ground and I would be the "climber," cutting all the branches of the tree. It was at this time that I met Grandma McCamish for the first time. I thought, "She is so precious!" Oh how she loves Jesus. She asked David, "Do you boys have insurance for this type of work?' David, "Sure do, John 3:16!" We all laughed as we walked into the back yard. The tree was tremendous. It was two, maybe even three times the height of the house. It has six major branches on it, and each one was larger around than my whole body.

We backed David's Toyota Truck into the backyard and 5 men from our church in Sun Valley began unloading the chainsaw, ropes, and equipment. I tied myself into the tree in such a way that I could swing out of the way of the limb as it was cut, without falling out of the tree. The plan was to make a "rope cradle" for each cut limb to rest in. Then lower it to the ground and cut it into small pieces. One end of the rope was tied to the back of David's truck and I took the other end and climbed to the top of the tree and threw the rope over the highest part of the tree. Then I tied it off at both ends of the limb I was cutting. As I cut each limb the ground shook, and the limb snapped and broke away from the tree, swaying like a baby in a cradle. Then we lowered it to the ground. The first five limbs were cut with no problem.

The last one was the largest, about 30 feet long and 2 feet around. As I cut this limb it fell upon a smaller branch which made it bounce out of the prepared cradle. It all happened so fast!! The back of the truck came off the ground and the limb came sliding down the branch where I had tied myself into the tree - my leg was laying in the crotch of the tree as this huge limb smashed into it. My leg popped, just like ice being crushed. David and the men couldn't see me anymore because the limb covered my body. The last thing they saw was the chainsaw running at full speed. David thought for sure that the chainsaw had cut into my stomach. Everyone jumped in the back of the truck trying to add weight to get the wheels of the truck on the ground again for traction, but it was no use. I was pinned in the tree about 7 feet above the roof of the house and no one could reach me. One man went to call the paramedics. The pain in my leg was so intense. I tried to cut myself out of the tree but the chainsaw jammed in the thick wood of the tree. I started yelling, "Praise You Jesus! Praise You Jesus! Praise Your Jesus! And then I got dizzy. My leg was swelling under the weight of the limb and I had become so weak. I laid my hand on the limb and said, "Oh God, please move this just a little bit so my leg can fall out." I heard a whisper in my ear, "50 men could not move this log, but I will move it with My finger." The log moved UP the branch it had slid down on. My leg fell out and the guys started shouting and crying with joy. They had seen a miracle of God.

I reached over to lower myself into the arms of my brother Manny Dealba on the roof; and he reached out and pulled me to himself on the roof. After a few minutes on the roof the paramedics came. They looked at the tree and then looked at me and said, "How did you get here on the roof?" I said God did not want to share the glory with you so He delivered me Himself. The paramedic put my leg in a splint and packed ices around it, and then took my pulse. It was 80 over 60 and they were surprised at the low pulse.

They took me to the hospital and took an x-ray of my leg and they were shocked to find that there were **no broken bones!** Even though I had heard the sound of crushed ice when the log smashed into my leg. God had healed my leg supernaturally. Oh, how I love You Jesus!

They released me that afternoon. I came back to see the tree finally cut down. That night I was not able to sleep because of the pain in my leg. I remember taunting the devil that night. "you're such a fool devil. you think you are hurting me by keeping me awake like this. All you're doing is keeping me awake so I can praise my God for delivering me, even more." I praised God and sang songs of worship until I fell asleep. The next day was Passover Sunday.

David said I could sit in the congregation if I wanted to and he would lead the song service. I wanted to let everyone know that there was no way I was going to let the devil have even a small taste of victory. I threw my crutch down and began to lead the song service. I told everyone, "If

I start shouting loud it's because the pain is so great; so, when the pain gets greater I'll just sing louder - Hallelujah! We had the greatest service that Sunday morning.

After a little more than one year the church had grown to just over 100. I felt that God had finished His purpose for me in Sun Valley and that I should now return to my church in Maywood. It was a very difficult thing for me to do, leaving these beautiful people that I had become a part of. What was really exciting however, was that after I left the church exploded to over 200 people within 6 months.

Back in the Maywood church I was serving as an usher where one of the great benefits was that I got to have time with my good friend and Assistant Pastor Robert Bloom. One morning as we were counting the offering, I told him that I felt I was backslidden. He started to laugh. He said, "Why do you think that, Billy?" I said that for the past several weeks I had not felt the presence of God when I came to church, when I go to Bible Study, or when I go to work each day. I feel like He is not with me anymore. Pastor Bloom's typical response was to take my inquiring mind to the Word of God and show me what the Bible said. He directed me to several scriptures and I rediscovered that the Christian Experience is a "Faith Walk." God was building and stretching my faith by taking me beyond my "feelings." I praise God for the many lives He has invested into my life to make me what He wants me to be. When I think of Pastor Neville, Pastor Bloom, Grandma Clarissa, and all the others; I praise God for these people He has used to bless and guide my life.

One Friday as I was shopping for groceries I felt a sudden pain in my abdomen. As I bent over it became even more intense. I had to stop my shopping and stagger out of the store bent over to my car. I got in my car and managed to get to the emergency room of the hospital. The doctor examined me and asked what I had eaten, and what my profession was. When I told him that I hadn't eaten anything recently and I was an accountant, he said that I was probably just under a little stress and that the pain will probably pass. He ordered x-rays and the x-rays did not show anything unusual. I was still in very great pain. My breath was coming in short gasps. He said that I would be alright and told me to go home. At home I was alone and in pain all night... all during the next day and into

Sunday morning. I was wondering how I could bear this pain anymore. On the other end of Los Angeles County, in Long Beach, Pastor Bloom and his wife Esther were on their way to church. God spoke to them and told them to call me. When they called I was trying hard not to cry. He said he would come over right away and take me to the hospital. When we arrived, he told the doctor that he knew me, and that I was not the kind of person to complain about pain unless it was really genuine. The doctor said that there was no evidence that there was anything wrong with me but agreed to ask for another doctor's opinion on this.

When the duty surgeon came in and touched the exact place of the pain, he shouted to the nurse, "Get this man up to OR immediately! He has a ruptured appendix." They put me on a bed and rushed me to an elevator. While I was waiting for the elevator to open, the pain, the gasping breath, the desperation all made me so tired. I called to the Lord and said, "Oh God, I'm too tired to fight for my breath anymore." I closed my eyes and everything went black.

I felt like I was floating in the air, rising up toward a sea of stars. It was so peaceful and free. The pain was gone. I kept rising higher and higher when suddenly I felt like I was in a great pool of water - and someone had pulled the plug out. I was spinning around and around, as I felt myself being lowered down, down, and then my eyes opened and I saw this nurse dressed in white staring down at me. I said, "Am I in heaven?" She laughed, "No, but you are a very lucky man. We thought we had lost you." The doctor said pieces of my appendix were strewn all through my body, and that my appendix had probably been ruptured for the last three days. I can't remember ever being so tired and exhausted as I was that day. I praise God that Pastor Bloom listened to the Spirit of God that morning.

# CHAPTER EIGHT

*Now What*

At the end of 1984 on a Friday afternoon my boss came into my office and said, "Wednesday afternoon we need you to be in Addis Ababa, Ethiopia; will you go?" I shouted, "I've been ready to go for four years now!" I was so excited as I drove to church that night. I waited in the parking lot for Pastor Neville to arrive. Before he got out of his van I was right there at his door. "Pastor, guess what happened to me today?" Not waiting for his response, I told him how I had been asked to go to Ethiopia; and before we reached the door of the church he said, "I believe that you need to go on this one Billy."

I was delirious with joy. I knew no one who was Ethiopian. I didn't know the language, the culture, or the people. All I knew was this was going to be a great adventure with the Holy Spirit; and I was ready.

My boss assigned me the task of overseeing the financial activities of the Ethiopian Famine Relief Program. My plan was to hire and train Ethiopian nationals to do this work. As they learned how to do the job, I would be free to pursue the vision God had given me for the evangelism and Christian development of Ethiopian believers throughout Ethiopia.

I stared out the window of my plane as we cruised over the Atlantic Ocean and began talking with God. "There's so much death and discouragement that I have heard about in Ethiopia. I feel so limited and humbled by this great need they have." I thought about the thousands of starving babies, and as I thought about them I saw a stream of little babies leading up into the heavens. At the end of the stream I saw a pair of huge arms opened up receiving them.

"See Billy, they are the fortunate ones, coming home to Me where there is no more hunger, pain, suffering, or tears." I was so encouraged with this new and fresh perspective. This would be an important reference point for me to rest upon throughout the coming years of very difficult ministry,

As I left the plane after landing I felt like someone had laid a 200-pound sack of cement upon my shoulders. The oppression, sense of hopelessness and anger was overwhelming. I saw soldiers everywhere, some looking like teenagers, and the people looking so empty. I did not even feel saved.

"What happened to my faith God?" God said, "Oh Billy, your faith is the same now as it was in America. The difference here is that the emotion, you thought was faith, has vanished like foam in a glass of soda. What you thought was great faith in America was actually very little faith mixed with a lot of emotion."

Now that my "foam" was gone, I was left with just enough faith to survive my Christian experience. God told me to stay in my room and pray; and not to preach on the streets. It's illegal to practice evangelism and Christian development of believers in Ethiopia because the Socialist government has declared this to be illegal. God told me that He would bring the people to me.

After six weeks of prayer there was a knock on my door. I answered the door and saw two young women standing there. They said that they had been praying with their family at home when God spoke to them with spiritual tongues and interpretation.

God's instructions to them was to "Go to Ethiopia Hotel, Room 107, where My servant Billy Hall will teach you the Word of God."

I was shocked! In amazement, I followed them to their home and our first home church was begun that evening in the little village of Gulaley, a suburb or Addis Ababa.

During the evening hours after work, I walked the roads covered with a large white cloth called a gabi (Gah-bee). I covered my head and tucked my hands inside to disguise myself as an Ethiopian; because foreigners were forbidden to be in these residential areas. I did not want to bring attention to the various underground churches so I travelled the small roads instead of the main roads when possible. During the day I walked without the gabi. After a while I began to sense the people I walked among, and became highly sensitive to my surroundings; one of the benefits of training in the Marine Corps. I normally walk fast, so this made it difficult was the security people to follow me in the day time. I rarely used a taxi, because walking helped me feel the people. God promised to *give me every place my feet walked* - so I walked everywhere!

One evening as I walked to the Gulaley meeting it began to rain heavily with great wind. I couldn't see in front of me and ended up getting lost in the dark and driving rain. I just kept walking and praying, "Holy Spirit please guide me to the meeting tonight." Eventually, I found myself on the right road to the little meeting house and quickly made my way to the wall surrounding the little house. Because of the weather, I didn't realize it was past the midnight curfew. This was a problem! A local kabele (Kah-beh-lay) soldier started yelling at me in the Amharic language of Ethiopia. I quickly tucked my head and arms inside my gabi; lowered my head and crouched down in a corner of the wall. I silently prayed, "Oh God, please deliver me from this man." The soldier kept yelling words I didn't understand and after a while just walked away. After he disappeared around the corner I quickly jumped on top and then over the 8-foot wall into the compound where the house was. We had an exciting meeting that night.

It wasn't long before we began to have all-night meetings in the Gulaley House Church. These meetings would begin at about 6 pm and last until 5 am the next morning. The service would begin with praise and worship singing, after that the preaching, then the altar call and special prayer. After all that personal testimonies were shared, with a fellowship time of breaking bread, and enjoying coffee and tea for 30 to 45 minutes. We would then start praising and worshiping Jesus again; repeating the service again. We would sleep from 5 am to 7 am and then go to work that day. All told, we would have 5 back-to-back services that night.

During one of our all-night meetings God did another amazing miracle. Shortly after midnight, as I was leading everyone in praise and worship, I saw a soldier standing outside one of the open windows. He was staring straight at me - eyeball to eyeball. I felt fear grip me and heard the devil's whisper, "Now you're finished fool, and you're going to jail and you'll never see these people ever again."

I kept on singing and turned away from looking at the soldier, as if no one was there. As I turned I saw him again on the other side of the house outside that open window, looking at me again. I looked away again and kept on singing, not wanting to alarm the people in the meeting. Our meeting continued all night long. In the morning I left after curfew and before daylight so I could be on the road before any of the neighbors knew that I had spent the night there.

It was two days later that the sisters from the Gulaley house church came to see me. They were beside themselves with joy as they told me the story of God's amazing miracle. "Remember out last all-night meeting, Billy? Well, the people next door to our house came to our house the next day and asked what we were doing last night. They had called the kabele soldier that night, and complained about our singing, and asked him to take us to jail for disturbing them; and for having this church meeting in their house. When the soldier went back to their house he told them he had climbed over our wall, walked all around our house, but had seen no one and heard no sound! He warned them at the same time, that if they ever called him again concerning our house, he would take them to prison."

I praised God for His miracle! He showed all of us that He Who makes the eye see can just as easily make the eye _not_ see. He Who makes the ear to hear can also make the ear _not_ hear. What a mighty God we serve!

As I walked to meetings the Holy Spirit told me the roads to take. I didn't always take the same route. He told me what roads to avoid and when to avoid them. Sometimes He told me not to go to a scheduled meeting because there were security police waiting to capture me. He would speak to the people at the meeting in spiritual tongues or give them a supernatural word of wisdom that I was not coming because of a security trap; and urged the people to continue on with the service.

Sometimes instead of traveling by foot, some groups would send someone to pick me up from a specific. They would tell me, "Stand at this place on the road, at this time, on this day, and a car will come to pick you up." As I stood at the appointed place at the appointed time, a car would come by and stop and open the door. I would get in and they would drive me off to the place where the service was. Many times I did not know <u>who the driver was or where the meeting was</u>. We changed the meetings many times and kept them moving from house to house to avoid detection. When we left the meetings we never left in groups of more than 3 at a time; spacing our departure to avoid notice by the neighbors. The services were continuous. As some were leaving others were coming.

I had hired local staff to do the work I was sent to do. As I trained them they were very quick learners. This enabled me to be free to pursue my mission assignment that God had given me.

My first convert was a 16-year-old young man named Mesfin. He and his friends were curious about this foreigner who walked everywhere in and out of the city. As we all walked together I talked about why I came to Ethiopia; to share the experience I had been enjoying with Jesus for the last 12 years of my life.

I remember the day Mesfin gave his life to Christ. We all met on Sunday morning, at a place about 2 kilometers from the place where I was staying. We walked together talking for about 8 kilometers until we came to a mountain. We followed an old donkey trail up the mountain, zig-zagging all the way to the top. There was a beautiful green slope on the other side of the mountain. As Mesfin and his friends laid down on the green grass, I began to tell them the story of Joseph from the Book of Genesis. At the end, I asked them - "Who wants to be a Joseph for

Ethiopia?" Mesfin said, "I will. I want to give my life to Jesus!" I led him to Christ. I was so thrilled!

As we walked those roads together backdown the mountain, I began to wonder how Jesus must have felt walking with His disciples. It felt like we were all walking with Jesus down that donkey path that day. I felt like I had been saved all over again, it was wonderful and fresh.

It wasn't long before Mesfin began to witness to others at school. He started Bible Study groups on his own. At one point he had 5 Bible Study groups at different locations on the school campus. During the semester break and the holidays he kept the new believers busy in the Bible Study. He took my New Believer lessons, which he had learned by heart, and put them on the inside walls of his straw hut where he lived. Everyone who visited him would read those lessons on the wall.

One evening Mesfin and I were sitting together in a truck (this was forbidden for foreigners and Ethiopians at this time). Mesfin asked me to pray for him to be baptized in the Holy Spirit. When I did, Jesus baptized him in the Holy Spirit. He started laughing, crying, shouting, and praising God in his new heavenly language. What a joy this was to see this life blossoming like ae of the Rose of Sharon, Jesus Christ.

I discipled new believers by walking with them. In this socialist culture, if an Ethiopian was seen walking with a foreigner they were immediately suspected of being counter revolutionary. The paranoia is so widespread that no one was allowed to sit still in a public place, except in a restaurant. If your car is parked on the road and you are seen sitting there alone or with someone, the soldiers would come and force you to move at gun point. There were no parks to relax and fellowship in, so the only means of counseling was to walk together, along the way.

One afternoon as I was walking with one of our evangelists, whose name was Beza, a security officer walked up to us and flashed his ID card identifying himself. He took the evangelists ID card and my Passport and asked me what I was doing. "I'm talking with my friend," I said. Where did you meet him? "Here in Addis," I said. Then he began to question Beza in Amharic. I knew enough Amharic to understand this officer was about to take my friend and brother to prison, for interrogation and "special treatment." He suddenly handed me back my Passport and said I was free to go. I said that I was not going anywhere without my friend. He insisted that I go, and I insisted that I wasn't going anywhere without Beza. Then he took my Passport and led us both away to his office. Now, a crowd of people started to gather around us, growing so large that it blocked traffic. The people were yelling at the security officer to let us go but he ignored them. As we reached the parking lot of the Security building a very tall Ethiopian came out of the building. He was dressed in a very expensive suit. He walked up to us briskly and grabbed Beza's ID card and my Passport from the Security officer, and gave them back to Beza and I. He then said to us softly, "You may <u>both</u> go now, and <u>you</u>, speaking harshly to the Security Officer, <u>come inside with me!</u>"

Water Baptism was always an exciting event during this time in Ethiopia. It too, was an illegal activity! I had recently walked by a remote lake, and I thought to myself as I passed; "this is an ideal place for us the baptize believers." But the people who managed the place were not agreeable to this. So instead of making this a church event I just personally rented a small hut on the edge of the water. Two weeks before the scheduled day I asked the people in one of our meetings, who had not been baptized - and who wanted to be baptized. Three people raised their hand, and so we began teaching on water baptism. I took their names and telephone numbers both at work and at home; they were Hirot, Elias, and David. I told them I would let each of them know when and where we would meet. It all had to be kept secret because of the constant scrutiny of local security officers; and also, to protect the security of the people who managed the "facility."

The day before our lake-side appointment, I called them at work and told them where to be at 5:45 AM. I told them also, "I will leave at 6:00 AM!" When I arrived at 5:40 the next morning, they were all there. They got into the truck saying, "Where are we going?" I said, "I'll tell you when we get there. If something happens along the way, like an accident, or if we're stopped by security people and questioned separately; you can't tell them what you don't know."

I took the back roads over the hills and entered the lake area. The guards were asleep. They were so excited as we slipped down into the cold water! One of the evangelist's and I took each of them separately and baptized them in the name of the Father, the Son, and the Holy Spirit. David was very big and tall. He was so big that when we laid him down in the water, we all fell in with him; and came up praising God. We all rejoiced quietly for God's Unspeakable Gift Jesus Christ! What an exciting time this was.

# CHAPTER NINE

*Here Comes The Promise*

By June 1st, I was nearly exhausted. For three months I had been preaching nearly every night in the various underground churches. I remember one Saturday afternoon when I was really tired and trying to sleep. I had been invited to preach in an all-night service that evening and I was asking God to please let me just cancel the meeting so I could sleep. He refused to leave me alone. I could not sleep and I became frustrated. I said to myself, "It's not fair God, I'm so tired and You won't leave me alone. Please God, let me sleep tonight."

I lost the argument as usual, gave up trying to sleep and left my room. Walking on the road to the pickup location, I was still complaining. While I stood there waiting for the car to come pick me up, I started to feel ashamed of myself for behaving this way. A little white VW Bug rolled up to where I was standing and opened the door. I climbed in and we drove off to the meeting place.

This little lady that was driving the car asked me what my favorite song was. I said, "Amlake Yeh Deregewen ega," and we began to sing this powerful praise and worship song that became known in our churches as "Billy's Testimony." Translated it means:
*When I think of all the miraculous things You have done for me, I can talk about them over, and over and over, and never finish talking about all the miracles You have done in my life.*

As we sand this song I experienced tremendous refreshment in my body and I was no longer tired. I was excited, renewed, and exploding with joy as we arrived at the house. Nearly 50 people were gathered there in a large room. They formed two complete circles around me as I began to preach and share my testimony with them. We had a wonderful time, singing, preaching, praying, and fellowshipping with God and one another. We finished our service at 5 am and slept until 7 am. They asked me to share some more and I spoke until about 10 am. Then we closed the service.

As I reached the front gate of the compound where the house was, one of the ladies in the meeting named Mulu, came to the gate at the same time. We started talking and walking in the same direction. I asked her what school she was attending and she said she was not going to school any more, she was working. She began to talk about her children and as she told me about them I heard a voice in my heart say, "This is <u>My</u> daughter and <u>your</u> wife." I was shocked, "Dear God, I can't receive this word now, we're having revival and I don't have time for this. This must be a distraction from the enemy, trying to mess with my mind.

The Holy Spirit began to remind me of the promises He had given me long ago concerning my wife. All the pieces came together in a rush. She <u>had</u> two children; a girl and a boy, and the <u>girl was older</u> than the boy. She had been married but her husband had been killed in an accident four years earlier.

I thought, as she spoke, "Oh how she loves You Lord! With a heart like that, truly Lord, I could spend the rest of my life with her; just because of her heart of love for You." I asked her when I could meet her and her children and she told me Thursday evening would be fine. She continued to walk with me for a while, then turned aside to visit a friend while I continued to walk to Gulaley, where I had another all-night service scheduled.

I was surprised with this sudden change of events. As I was walking Holy Spirit was putting the sermons together that I would be preaching at the next service.

After the service I returned to my room still wondering about this incredible answer to prayer. "Wow God, You really do answer prayers in unexpected ways, don't you? When I least expect it and in the most unexpected way. I went to sleep that night thinking I would sleep for a week! The next morning I was immediately wide awake and working diligently at my job.

The following night there was no service scheduled. I had a good sleep. The next morning as I was praying, God instructed me that when I arrived at Mulu's house I was to tell her, "God has given you and your household to me and He commanded me to give you this $600.00."

I thought, "But God, what if she doesn't accept what I tell her? What if she slaps my face? I mean she doesn't even know me, except for a short walk we had together." He never responded to my anxious questioning. So, when Thursday evening came, Mulu came to the Ethiopia Hotel to meet me. We walked together all the way to her house, 1 mile away in village of Kera. Our friend Alemseged MeKonnen was there. I played with the children until late that night, after curfew; so, I ended up sleeping on the couch in her living room.

It was the next morning when I finally told her what God had instructed me to say to her. She immediately dropped to her knees and started crying and praising God for seeing her very deep and desperate need. She began telling me how God had been talking to her about me as well, and she too had refused to accept it.

She told me that she had not had money to pay the rent for her house for the last 5 months and was completely without food for the house. She was in desperate need for those finances and God gave her more than she needed. I was really thrilled to hear as she related her testimony to me. As she spoke my heart was burning, and I knew without a doubt that God was moving in this event.

We agreed together that we would pray and fast for a week and wait for the peace of God. God's peace will be His witness that this is His perfect will for us to marry. At the end of that week we still had no desire to marry each other, but we did have a deep and sure peace in our heart. So, by faith, we agreed to receive each other as a gift from God; and we set our wedding date.

In Ethiopia, it <u>is no simple thing</u> to get married. Permission is required from the local kebele (government official) for everything! To move from your house, to quit or change your job, to buy a sheep for celebration, to get a driver license, and also to get married.

When I went to see the city official in Addis Ababa, the lady said, "you have only been in Ethiopia for 6 months. You must be here at least one year with a clear record of good conduct, before we can consider allowing you to marry one of our women."

We had already prayed and set the date; now the enemy was going to try and keep this glorious wedding from happening. I asked God to do things His way in spite of these people. One of our Christian brothers,

Yosef, spoke with a government official and the date God gave us was finally made official.

The government of Ethiopia does not recognize church weddings, only civil ceremonies performed at the City Hall (Municipality). We went to the Municipality with all our guests on August 10, 1985. We registered our names and waited for the couple before us to be married. We stood up together when it was our turn, and the lady who had previously denied us permission *sent her representative* to perform the wedding.

Our guests met with us in the main meeting room in the Municipality, where we had a great praise and worship time. We sang the victory song, which translated says: "Praise God, You, have won the victory and satan is ashamed." There had never been a Christian Praise and Worship time in this Municipality since the communists took power in 1976. So, once again we all knew "That His right hand and His holy arm, hath gotten Him the victory." So, we sang unto the Lord a new song! Hallelujah!

Two months ater on October 25, 1985 we were married in the Church; Gulaley Bethel Mekane Yesus. Our wedding was performed according to the Ethiopian culture which is much the same as in the Old Testament days. It is one of the few occasions when the government will allow believers to gather together: because they believe the people are gathered together for a "wedding" and not a "church service;" *although a wedding necessarily involves a church service.*

That morning began at 8 am with my 4 best men and several of my friends meeting together with me in my room. In Ethiopian culture, the best men and their counter-parts, the best ladies; are committed to be a part of your life as husband and wife, as long as you live.

After we waiting for about 30 minutes for everyone who was invited to arrive, we left for the bride's house. Some were already walking to her house, and some were in the caravan of cars with me on our way to her house in Kera.

When we arrived, I got out of the car and the men gathered around me. They began leading me to and then through the small front gate to the house.

Her "ladies in waiting," were waiting eagerly inside along with many of their friends. We came into the house with myself in the lead. I saw Muluyey sitting on a small couch with our two children, Tsega and Henok, sitting on each side of her; and I began to weep. Her beauty and God's Promises fulfilled in my eyesight was too much to hold inside anymore. I kissed her cheek and the faces of our precious children. From that moment on I couldn't stop smiling. I was so very happy.

My friends at World Vision had promised to take the pictures and video of our wedding day, so I didn't ask anyone else to take pictures. When my friends from World Vision were unable to come I was frustrated and discouraged. It was now time for another unexpected miracle of God. A friend of mine, Mike Cunfa, was prompted by God the night before to come and take pictures of our wedding day.

After about an hour of taking pictures at the house, we left for the lunch area. The caravan following us grew much larger as more people came to join us and our bus, which was full to capacity. By the time we reached the garden of Ethiopia Mesk there were about 150 people with us. We all ate together and more pictures and video were taken.

About 2:00 in the afternoon we left with the caravan for the Church in Gulaley. When we arrived there the church was filled to capacity, except for the front 6 rows, which had been reserved for our bridal party. The church held 2,200 people! Folks were standing outside and speakers were set up so they could all hear the ceremony.

The church was so beautiful inside. High ceilings made the praise and worship echo like thunder - I felt as though the ceiling was going to open up at any moment, and God was going to rapture us all straight up into heaven! The choir then sang three songs and the pastor of the church performed the Ethiopian Wedding Ceremony. I spoke my vows in Amharic, the native language of Ethiopia, and the people shouted with joy! As we exchanged our rings, the pastor asked us each to take a candle and light the one unity candle in the center of the platform. He asked us to go to opposite ends of the platform, and then meet in the middle where we lit the candle. He told the massive congregation: Ethiopia shall go up at one end," pausing and pointing first to one side, "and America shall go up at the other end:" gesturing to the other side, "and they <u>shall</u> become one here in the middle." The people shouted with a great shout! It was glorious!

After we lit the unity candle with each of our candles, I took the microphone and began to share my testimony of God's promise to me 12 years earlier of giving me a wife, and how this day, God's promise was fulfilled in their eyesight and their hearing.

The service ended at 5:00 pm and we had a reception in the garden area of the church outside until 6:30 pm. As people began to leave, we spent the early evening with the brothers and sisters of our fellowship. When everyone else was gone, we were invited by our brother Getachew and sister Yeshiareg to spend three days and two nights in their home. We accepted their invitation. That night we had an unbelievable wonderful praise and worship season with the Lord, and our friends, celebrating this miracle that He had done among us. It lasted until nearly midnight. We were exhausted with joy!

World Vision had arranged a place for us to live. Their policy was to give expatriates like myself, 10 days of rest and recuperation every three months. Due to the intense work of hiring and training national staff, I was unable to take advantage of my rest and recuperation leave for almost a year. So, the organizations leadership decided to give us a delayed honeymoon and bought round-trip tickets to Mombasa, Kenya for 10 days. We had a great time.

When we came back home the company further decided that since I had not been able to rest during my tour of duty as others had, they bought our whole family round-trip tickets to America for an extended vacation. I did not realize how crucial these tickets would be to us later on.

Our ministry continued to blossom as Muluyey and I continued to serve the home Bible Study groups, and saw God continue to save, deliver, and build His people. God was moving again to fulfill His promise to me. You see, our family was beginning to grow; Muluyey had become pregnant. The months that followed were exciting and full of hope and promise. But as always, "blessing never comes without a fight;" sometimes to the death

# CHAPTER TEN

## *The Birth of Joanna*

The night Muluyey was to be delivered, her water bag broke at about 1:00 am in the morning. This was really tough because there was a midnight to 6am curfew in Ethiopia that was severely enforced at this time. I thought, "Dear God, why couldn't this happen before midnight or after 6am?" Despite the curfew, I simply had to get my wife to the hospital. I prayed; "God, please move the soldiers out of our way!"

I helped her into the truck and charged off down the road to the hospital. It seemed like a popular place when we arrived, as they told us there were no beds available. Unbelievable! I saw ladies lying on stretchers everywhere; pregnant and ripe for delivery, some with babies delivered and umbilical cords still attached! I thought, "This is Crazy!"

Some woman in the delivery area heard there was a Christian woman who needed a bed, and this woman gave up her bed for Muluyey - the woman stayed in the delivery area. Little did we know how this would be a matter of life and death in the end.

Muluyey had been complaining about sharp stabbing pains throughout her body all morning from 2am to 8:30 am when the resident doctor came in on his morning rounds. This was the same doctor who had delivered her two previous children by performing a C-Section. He was very upset when he learned that Muluyey had not been operated on to deliver the baby prior to his arrival at the hospital that morning. Especially in light of her patient history!

Immediately, they rushed her into surgery, but they told me they could not operate until they had at least two pints of blood. This was due to a critical shortage of blood in the hospital at that time. The hospital staff told me where I could pick up this blood from, so I raced over to the other hospital. God had a Christian sister there that got the blood for me immediately! I raced back to the hospital where Muluyey was, just as they delivered the blood to the hospital. I was told to wait outside the operating room until the doctor came out.

When he finally came out he grimly told me that Muluyey was bleeding heavily and they could not control it. There was more bad news; her bladder had ruptured, her uterus had ruptured, and the baby was dead. Ny heart was crushed, and time seemed to stand still. He said all they could do was close her up and hope the bleeding would stop. It was then that a lady darted out of the operating room carrying a bloody mass into the elevator out of my sight.

I cried out in anguish and pleaded, "God, please don't let the devil have this victory. I've waited twelve years for this miracle and now satan is trying to kill both my wife and Your baby." "I rebuke this death, in Jesus Name," were the words that came out of my mouth at that moment. I <u>must</u> have seemed like a mad man those who were looking at me, not understanding my English.

I just sobbed as I struggled to get back to her room. They brought her into me unconscious. Her catheter bag was filled with bright red blood. I crawled up on her bed next to her in the fetal position; "Muluyey, see how God healed the woman with an issue of blood . . . see how He raised the dead man Lazarus . . . He will raise you and our Joanna . . . please Muluyey, don't die!" I knew I was preaching to myself as well as to Muluyey.

The next day the catheter bag turned from being red-orange to orange. The second day it turned from yellow-orange to yellow. On the third day Muluyey regained consciousness and began babbling incoherently. It was then that they brought Joanna's tiny body into the room. She was bleeding from her nose, ears, eyes, and mouth. A nurse had seen her movement among the dead babies in the basement. By the end of this third day Joanna's bleeding had completely stopped. Oh, how I love that "third day." That third day is always pretty tough on the devil, don't you know!

After 10 days I walked out of the hospital holding Muluyey with one arm and Joanna in the other arm. The English speaking nurses said, "Look at this dead woman walking - and listen to this dead baby crying; their God has done this, the impossible, for them!"

They marked Muluyey's room as the "Miracle Room;" because of what God had done, and what some kind stranger in the delivery room had done - giving up her bed for a stranger in need. Little did that stranger know at that time, that the lady in need was her very own cousin. That's right, the stranger turned out to be Muluyey's cousin Lekaylesh Worku.

The birth of our child Joanna was another of God's promises fulfilled in the most difficult of circumstances. Not surprising though, we serve the God of the impossible.

Now over the months, ministry and growth had not stopped. In fact, the work became so prominent that it began to be a threat to the government. What soon followed was impossible to anticipate.

## CHAPTER ELEVEN

*Out of Ethiopia*

To make a very long story short it was through a series of unique events involving the communist government officials and my employer that I became unemployed in May 1986; shortly after Joanna was born.

As an American with no employment my visa automatically expired. I was suddenly an "illegal alien" in this communist country. I had a wife and children that I needed to get out of this country as well. The Immigration authorities said they would give everyone EXCEPT Joanna a visa (permission to leave the country). Joanna would have to stay behind. This is the typical strategy for communist countries, to separate families; holding one or more family members hostage, insuring that the rest of the family will return to Ethiopia. Well, that was not going to happen to this Marine's family; not on my watch!

So, we prayed and waited for God to do another miracle. I had 4 round trip tickets to America, which I had saved from the rest and recuperation benefits package from my employer. I only needed to buy one ticket for Joanna. We had so little money but we bought the ticket anyway. The airline tickets were set to expire on July $3^{rd}$ which was a Sunday. It was now July $2^{nd}$, Saturday. We still did not have our exit visas. Saturday is a working day in Ethiopia, until 12 noon. Shortly before noon, one of our Christian brothers who working in the Immigration Department; went to the official's office with our visa applications. The official was sitting there signing a stack of applications hurriedly, so he could go home that day. Our applications were placed in the stack, and were signed hurriedly along with the rest of the applications. Hallelujah!

The next morning which was Sunday we boarded the plane and still felt the tension of the situation. We felt that we would soon be discovered. Furthermore, our children and Muluyey had never been in an airplane before and they were scared. All this was so new to ALL of us. As the plane lifted off the ground we all were so happy and relieved.

Oh God, once again, You, made a way where there was no way. You are my

Miracle, Jesus! We were off to another chapter, which God was beginning to write with our lives both individually, and collectively as a family. America was about to become the next chapter in our life, which would add to the testimony of *God's Amazing Love!*

It was July 7$^{th}$, 1986 when we landed at LAX (Los Angeles International Airport). After 4 hours in US Customs, we walked out and were met with the smiles and greetings of my good friends, and Bible Study Leaders, Bill and Marlene Beveridge. It was great but somehow also very strange. In was like being on another planet for all of us. I felt like a tourist in my own homeland, America. I was totally out of touch with Los Angeles. I had become an Ethiopian for the past 1 ½ years and now my new family and I were visitors on vacation. A much needed vacation for sure.

It is such a wonderful experience to be a recipient of all the blessings unfolded by God in our family and ministry. Los Angeles was to be no different! The first place we went to was a hotel, which had a swimming pool. My family had never seen so much water in one place. I threw the kids into the water and then yelled as I jumped in with them. Joanna was only 6 weeks old and I took her into the pool with us. She swam like a professional, without lessons. I guess she thought she was still in the little swimming pool of Muluyey's tummy.

It was not long before my ministry friends found out about my return to the States. Soon I was asked by Pastor David to come back to Sun Valley and help him as his assistant pastor. He had many new converts but not many leaders to disciple among these growing Christians. So we rented a little place in the City of Sunland. We all enjoyed this "little city in a country" style environment. The mountains have often reminded us of our homeland in Northern Ethiopia.

The weeks and months passed by as I led our family into this new chapter in our life together. That September came and the children started school in the second and third grade. I spent the evenings with them translating their homework and helping them to understand the English directions for their homework.

Muluyey applied for admission to a computer word processing college. The Administrator gave her an English

Comprehensive Test, which she failed. Rather than walk away in defeat she turned to the Administrator and said, "If you let me come to this college, I will be the best student here." The Administrator was so impressed. She couldn't understand how Muluyey would be able to understand the instructors without having satisfactory comprehension of the English language. However, she agreed to accept Muluyey into the college.

Now, during the evenings I helped my wife and children in their studies. I bought a tape recorder for Muluyey. I told her to take it to class and record the instructor. When she brought it home we discussed all that the instructor had said. Muluyey became the kind of student she promised the Administrator she would be by graduating as the top student in her class.

## CHAPTER TWELVE

*What Has God Done*

I was so very proud of my family. They have all done so very well in their studies. It has all been with God's help and by His design. But what now?

Not long ago a friend of mine asked me, "Billy, what is the next thing with you and God? What do you think God has *up His sleeve* for you guys after all you have been through . . . everything that you have learned?"

I knew it was coming, you know the question, What Has God Done? But when he asked me, I had to smile. I remember those times as a little boy when God spoke to me and said that I would preach His Gospel.

I remember when He spoke to me in my prison cell and spoke again to me concerning the things to come into my life.

I remember His promise to bring me a wife, and a family.

I remember His questions penetrating my mind rapidly, like machine gun fire. "Did you ever wonder why you survived all the killing in Vietnam - Do you know what it's like to live in a communist country? Do you ever why you passed through these years in prison - Do you know what it's like to be in a communist prison?

I remember His call, "I have called you to the communist nations; I am giving you East Germany, Poland, Hungary, Yugoslavia, Czechoslovakia, Romania, Bulgaria, Russia, China, and Ethiopia; there are your babies! Pray for them as a father prays for his children. I will break the back of communism and the world will know that I the Lord God have done this work."

I remember the day the wall in East Germany fell, and I was not surprised at all. I remember His miracles performed out of His great heart of love and compassion.

Never has it been so easy for me, and the thousands He has called to traverse the Globe, and tell of His unfailing promises. I know exactly where I am going! I'm going to tell others of *His Amazing Love!*

Made in the USA
Columbia, SC
14 July 2022